up in smoke

up in smoke

jonathan futrell + lisa linder

conran
OCTOPUS

First published in 1998 by
Conran Octopus Limited
37 Shelton Street
London WC2H 9HN

Conceived and produced by **LB Publishing Ltd.**

Photography, Text and Design copyright
© LB Publishing Ltd 1998

Photography* and Art Direction: Lisa Linder
Author: Jonathan Futrell
Editor: Hilary Burden
Designer: Lucy Gowans
Picture Researcher: Cheryl Newman
Assistant Picture Researcher: Jackie Montague
Book Co-ordinator and Researcher: Christina Wilson
Sub-editor: Chris Gill
Production Controller: Julian Deeming

British Library Cataloguing-in-Publication Data
A catalogue record for this book
is available from the British Library
ISBN 1-85029-987-0

Printed in China

(* except pages 6, 80-113)

contents

6 Introduction:
going up in smoke
The renaissance of cigar smoking

10 The holy grail:
Cuba
Back to the roots of the world's finest cigars

46 Spreading the seed:
going global
Central America, the Caribbean, Miami-a world of cigars

78 Power & passion:
movie moguls and revolutionaries
Cigars that shaped the world

114 Burning desire:
where there's smoke there's style
The modern smoker

142 The right stuff:
lighting up and the paraphernalia
Doing it right and knowing when to stop; cigar etiquette

158 The knowledge:
is size everything?
Length, girth, colour and taste; what's yours?

176 Clubbing:
a world of cigar lounges
Travels with a humidor. From Notting Hill to LA,
a bar fly's guide

190 Acknowledgments, Glossary & Index

in what must be the rehabilitation phenomenon of the century, cigars are back - and big business.

While anti-smoking forces in Europe and the USA have cigarettes on the run, cigars have neatly side-stepped the attacks, returned from the sales slump of a decade ago, and emerged largely unscathed - not just more popular than ever, but a necessary decadence.

For the first time in the history of cigar smoking, what was once the parodied face of affluence is now a symbol of refinement, albeit with a dash of humour. What the personal organizer was to the 1980s, and the mobile telephone was to the 1990s, the hand-rolled cigar is to the second millennium - an essential part of the good life for those prepared to enjoy it.

Actors, rock-and-roll icons, designers, fashion models and other members of the new glitterati have taken to cigars in a big way, and most are more than happy to put up their hand and be photographed; their new-found passion poised tantalizingly close to their lips. Their faces stare out at us from covers of magazines, published to foster and promote the cigar phenomenon we set out to explore here.

From Paris to Los Angeles, and from London to Havana, photographer Lisa Linder and I have met people with an unbridled passion for cigars - and life. Musicians and film directors, media commentators and designers regaled us with tales of their favourite smokes; how they harboured their secret desire for years, only outing themselves recently, thanks to the new social acceptability of cigars. We spoke with the people who market and sell them, and we sat and smoked in the clubs, or divans, where cigar people retire at the end of the day.

We travelled to Third World Dominican Republic, risking life and limb in a rental car without brakes, to discover how the Young Turks are modernizing production and coping with demand. And finally, we went to Cuba to meet the people, touch the soil and breathe the warm tropical air which together form the source of cigar mythology.

In a peculiar way our journey resembled meeting members of an unofficial, worldwide club, a sort of secret society dedicated to pleasure. Everyone seemed to know - or at least know of - the person we had spoken with days before, in another continent. Even if they had never met, each knew of the other's reputation; of their particular function in the global community of cigars. Through a world of elegant bohemians with a taste for tobacco, we were able to embrace and enjoy the traditions and rituals of cigars.

But it is not all lip-gloss and attitude; sales figures speak for themselves. From the start of the cigar boom in the early 1990s we have witnessed a fourfold increase in the world's appetite for premium hand-rolled cigars, whether from Cuba or elsewhere.

We are not dealing here with inexpensive, factory-rolled 'short-fill' cigars, more often than not made with the tobacco that premium cigar makers reject. (Open one up and the insides consist of shavings). The modern passion is almost exclusively for genuine, hand-rolled cigars. Pull one of those beauties apart and you will find whole tobacco leaves running the entire length to facilitate a smooth, unimpeded flow of smoke. They are wrapped and bound in more leaves, cultivated with diligence and care by farmers who understand the complex relationship between natural forces and flavour, then rolled in factories by nimble hands, in a process that has barely changed for centuries. Who could fail to be seduced by that?

As habits go, puffing on cigars is not a cheap one to sustain, especially if your fancy is for one of the revered Cuban brands. Yet, like the oenophile, unable to shake off a thirst for rare Burgundian wine, so the true devotee is prepared to pay handsomely for a box of genuine Havanas. Nevertheless, cigar production is booming in the Dominican Republic, Honduras, Nicaragua, Jamaica and elsewhere in the tropics, and just as wine drinkers have adapted to New World blends, so the cigar lover is learning to embrace a different - and invariably cheaper - kind of smoke.

New cigar factories have opened in many countries while, across the globe, the retail side of the industry has experienced a corresponding expansion, and, with that, the emergence of another phenomenon - the cigar club.

Cigar smokers are a breed apart; they enjoy the ritual of cigars (cutting, charring, lighting, smoking - talking cigars, too) and places like The No.1 Cigar Club in London, Cibar in New York, the Grand Havana Room in Los Angeles and Cheroots in Kuala Lumpur are havens for lovers of this absorbing new passion.

Clearly the cult of the cigar is here. It is looking good, and it is in excellent company. **JF**

the holy grail

Nothing brings out the best in Cubans quite so convincingly as a good cigar.

Making your way through customs at Havana's Jose Marti Airport, the smell of tobacco is the first thing that hits you, after the distinctive slap of moist Cuban heat. Our taxi driver has a stogie pressed into his face for the entire duration of the drive into downtown Havana. We pass motorcyclists, hitch-hikers, old men watching the day and a policeman changing the wheel of his squad car - each one is smoking a cigar.

This is a special day. Cigar people from all over the world are gathering at the Habana Libre Hotel for the annual Cigar Festival week. It's the cigar world's Academy Awards, where aficionados are invited to enjoy three of the year's finest smokes.

TV crews trip over themselves, searching for the famous, chasing actor Matt Dillon to his seat at the front of the stage; old friends, colleagues and rivals in the cigar business back-slap and outdo each other with impressive custom-rolled stogies.

The national cigar company, Habanos, uses these dinners to reward success and launch new brands. Tonight the main feature is the Trinidad Fundador, a cigar roughly the same size as a Cohiba Lancero, at 7½in. long, but a little thicker, with a ring gauge of 40. It has never previously been for sale and, it was said, was only produced in limited numbers as a diplomatic gift. Some government voices had even denied its existence. However, with many major Cuban brands registered with powerful USA corporations who are ready to pounce if the trade embargo is lifted, the decision was taken to make Cuba's most mysterious cigar available to the general public, and launch it in typical flamboyant style.

Another of today's objects of desire is the Cuaba. A strange looking beast, tapered at both ends, it was designed specifically for the British market and made to resemble the cigars of the 19th century. But it is the third choice that catches my eye, the Vegas Robaina, a cigar brand with the unique distinction of being named after a living Cuban. Such a tribute is unprecedented and would have been unthinkable in earlier revolutionary times, but things are changing fast in Cuba and the rules are being broken all the time.

robaina

So Vegas Robaina is the brand, and Robaina himself (pictured left) is now at centre stage, graciously receiving the Tobacco Grower of the Year award. A small, frail, 80-year-old man, with white cropped hair and skin like caramelized parchment, his words of gratitude are drowned out by applause. He bows and leaves.

To discover the reason for such adulation and to try to unravel some of the secrets, the myths and the hearsay of Cuban tobacco production, we set out the next day in a hire car, equipped with the most basic tourist map of the country, and head west to Pinar del Rio.

Havana's suburbs around the Miramar, *en route* to the motorway, look like Beverly Hills in need of garden maintenance - modernist and hacienda-style homes, avenues of palm trees and walls thick with bougainvillea. In old Havana, 19th century homes are collapsing in the middle of the night from years of neglect, but out here all is elegant and secure; the soldiers on every drive see to that.

Cuba is 1250km (777 miles) from east to west and 191km (119 miles) at its widest, from north to south, and it boasts five tobacco-growing regions: the Vuelta Abajo; the Semi Vuelta; Partidos; Remedios and Oriente. Each produces a quality of tobacco that other countries can only observe with envy. Yet only one, the Vuelta Abajo, in the region of Pinar del Rio, about three hours' drive south-east of Havana, produces leaves for all three component parts of the basic hand-rolled Cuban cigar (see page 34). This is the Côte Rôtie of the Rhone Valley, the Manzanilla of sherry; the source of Havana's finest; the Holy Grail. Here the soil is a livid hue of terracotta and for the cultivation of cigar tobacco, the combination of temperature and prevailing winds is un-rivalled anywhere in the world.

If you want to be sure of growing the best tobacco for the finest cigars, you need a farm in the Vuelta Abajo, as close to the city of Pinar del Rio, in the province of the same name, as possible. Naturally, this is where you will find Alejandro Robaina.

The drive east, across a flat, uneventful land, towards the Rosario Mountains, is remarkable for many things, not least the almost total absence of traffic in either direction. Bare-backed teenagers ride mopeds on the wrong side of the road; groups of hitchhikers are huddled beneath unfinished bridges leading to nowhere; and every mile or so, smiling farm workers wave at us with fronds of fresh garlic. We don't buy but they seem content with a wave in return.

From the terrace of the Los Jazmines Hotel, an elaborate pink edifice to the north of Pinar del Rio, at Vinales, we begin to sense the excitement most aficionados experience when first laying eyes on these tobacco fields. It is one of the most beautiful sights I have ever seen: serene and bountiful; a craggy valley of verdant granite monuments, towering above tobacco farms, and a portrait of Cuban life that can barely have changed for hundreds of years.

It is February, and midway through the harvest. Tobacco plants throughout the Vuelta Abajo are tall and succulent. People toil in almost every field we pass. Milky white oxen draw sleds of picked leaves and now and then we come upon dark-skinned men on horseback, their faces shaded by wide brimmed

hats. Each one is smoking a cigar. The only buildings for as far as we can see are *casas del tabacos*, the pitch-roofed drying sheds.

Taking the road to San Luis, we had been told to turn left at the brow of the first hill, on to the dirt road, by a sign that read 'Bien Venedo a la CCS VietNam Heroico' (Welcome to the Heroes of Vietnam Co-operative).

We follow this bumpy track into a valley and around past a flamboyan tree, bearing long dangling seed pods. Children and old folk emerge from wooden shacks to watch us bump and clank past their homes. Another flamboyan tree, some giant cacti and discarded oil drums; and as we approach, chickens disperse in a fright of feathers. We press on through a broken-down car-repair yard, where both engines and buildings have given up the ghost, lying dead in the heat. Then right at a school house, through an avenue of tobacco and into Vegas Robaina.

For such a living legend, Don Alejandro Robaina leads a humble existence. The land has been in his family since his grandfather bought it in 1845 and he personally took over the running of the farm from his father in the 1940s. The single storey house is squat and basic; a verandah on three sides gives on to shady rooms, their walls adorned with photographs of Robaina's five children.

Don Alejandro shares the house with his sister, Marise, and his two most prized possessions, a pair of antique wind-up gramophones and a stack of 78rpm records. Over there, a picture of Pope John Paul, here some glass ornaments. He offers me a *puros*, the cigar equivalent of moonshine, rolled by one of his farm hands that morning.

'A lot of people come here; they want to take a picture of themselves with me for a souvenir,' he says. 'There was an American actor who had been in seven films. He was a fat man but I don't remember his name. There are ambassadors from Canada and Nicaragua, others from Africa and bankers from Spain.'

Don Alejandro Robaina has been Cuba's top tobacco grower for almost two generations. His leaves are used by several prestige Habanos brands, including Cohiba, and they can be found inside or wrapped around most top-of-the-range double coronas. When Cuba's entire harvest was very nearly wiped out by blue mould in 1979, Don Alejandro's skill not only kept the mould at

the key is in knowing when to pick the tobacco.

If the *veguero* picks too early the cigar will not be good and it is the same even a day too late.

bay, it even helped increase his yield. Since 1997, though, when the range of four Vegas Robaina cigars was launched amid a fanfare of publicity in Madrid, Cuba's old man of tobacco has become a *bona fide* celebrity.

'Che's Guevara's brother came here, but the second time he came I couldn't receive him. I was too busy with visitors.'

Fame suits him well. He is at the top of his profession, outspoken and proud, a maverick in a process that has hardly changed for five centuries.

'For me the key is in knowing when to pick the tobacco. If the *veguero* picks too early the cigar will not be good and it is the same even a day too late. You have to take the leaf at the precise moment - and it is not easy to know either. Why do you think I have all this white hair?

'The state has never interfered in the way I cultivate my tobacco. For example, I am the only farmer in Cuba not to use a plough and turn the soil upside down. Instead I use discs to cut the soil and preserve the vegetable layer of the land, as it has always been. I learnt this from my father.

'He taught me never to break a leaf; they should be taken off complete and not damaged. And if you put too much fertilizer around the plant the leaf will burn, because when they move the land around the tobacco to remove the weeds, some of it lands on the leaf and the taste can be destroyed by the chemicals. Also, when you take off the flower, if you do it badly you will destroy the plant. So many things to remember...

'That is why I have had the best results of the country and I can prove it - in quality and quantity, setting new national and international records. The state used to plant tobacco 12 inches apart and now they will plant it 14 inches so the leaf will grow bigger. That is because this is how I grow it. Really, you have to go even bigger, you have to move the plants further apart for better leaves.

'This is why I think I deserve to have my name on a cigar. Other brands can't talk. Trinidad can't talk, H.Upmann can't talk, Cohiba can't talk. Not one of the other brands can talk. But Vegas Robaina can talk... the brand is alive and talking to you.

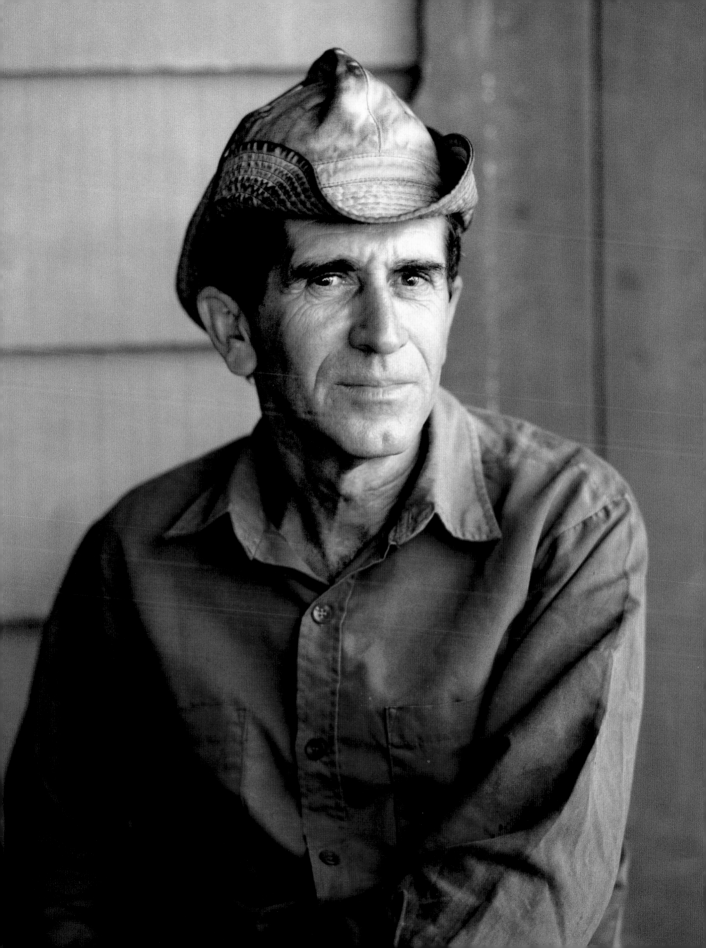

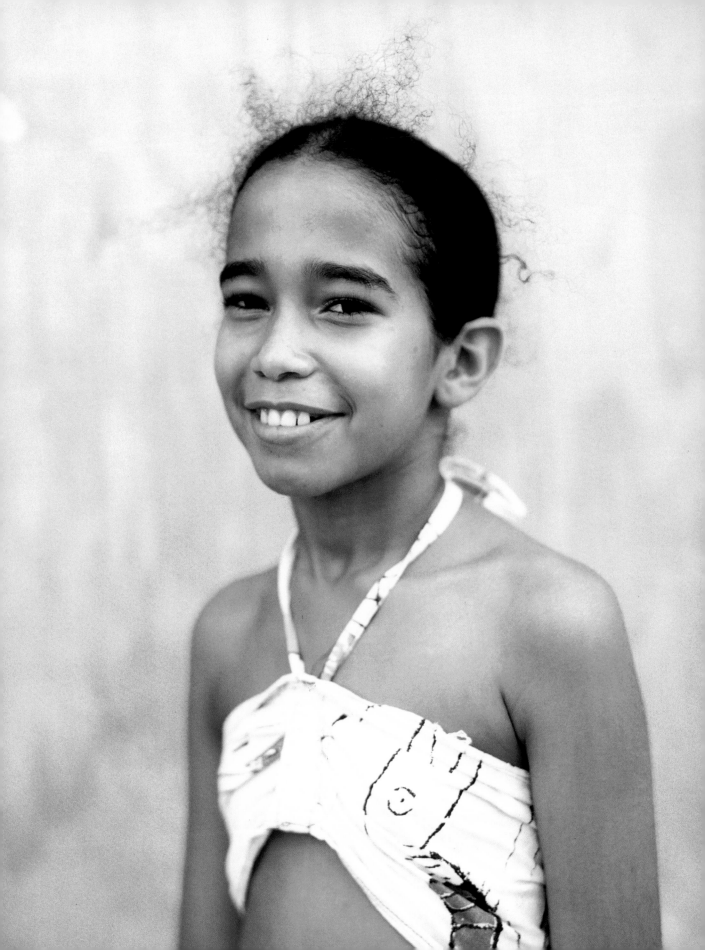

It is our last night in Pinar del Rio and all I want to do is drink rum and smoke cigars.

'five boxes of my cigars were sent to Fidel, each signed by me. He said to give them to the President of the Cuban parliament because he doesn't smoke anymore. Nowadays I know he talks a lot about me. He wants to cut me into pieces to make a lot of other men who can grow tobacco like me.'

After a second cup of coffee Don Alejandro shows us around the farm, to the fields of *corojo*, covered in tent-like sheets of muslin to protect the treasured *capa* leaves, tended by men on stilts. Then to his newest *casa del tabaco*. There I meet Maria Louisa, one of several women who use long needles to sew together hands of eight leaves which are hung on poles, called *cujes*, to dry. She prefers it here in the shade rather than in the field and she works fast - perhaps aided by the glass of rum at her side - her fingers bound with strips of fabric for protection against the needle. On a good day she can sew as many as 10,000 tobacco leaves.

'You see, Robaina is made with a lot of love and a lot of tears,' says Don Alejandro.

The journey back to Havana is the most fraught of my life. It is not enough that the motorway is unlit at night and our hire car is without a main beam, or

Page 22: José Trevilla with a freshly rolled 'puros' cigar.
Pages 23-30: harvesting in Pinar del Rio.

that the roadside is crowded with hitchhikers. There is another, even more terrifying, hazard: cattle. After a day spent grazing there is nothing the cows of Pinar del Rio like more than to sleep awhile on the warm tarmac of the Autopista Habana, oblivious to the fact that, on average, so I'm told, a speeding car slams into the flank of a sleeping heifer at the rate of one a week.

But we have no choice. The cigar factories are concentrated in Havana and our appointment at El Laguito, home of the Cohiba and now the enigmatic Trinidad, is first thing in the morning. Praying that the local cows are all wide awake, I step on it.

Cuba's most lauded cigar, the Cohiba (not its best seller though, that remains the Montecristo) has been produced at the El Laguito factory since the 1960s. According to legend, Fidel Castro was so enamoured of the taste of the home-rolled variety, smoked by one of his security guards, he decided to establish the factory in an elaborate 1920s, Italianate mansion on the outskirts of Havana (formerly the home of an English sugar cane magnate). This way, he could enjoy them himself, as well as impress visiting dignitaries.

the factory was created by our Commander In Chief and it was made with the idea of giving jobs to women.

The President chose the sizes he enjoyed best - the lancero, the corona especiale and panetela - and had their creator and blender, Eduardo Ribera, supervise production. It seems only right that El Laguito should have been chosen to produce the Trinidad, the cigar that has usurped the Cohiba as the ultimate symbol of Cuban diplomatic courtesy.

El Laguito is unlike any other factory I know, in the accepted sense of the word. The lemon and verdigris walls, the coiled staircase and stained glass, the ornate architraves and ceiling mouldings and the tall, shuttered windows are more suggestive of the world of opera than of a means of production. With the exception of a lift, to move the bales of tobacco, the mansion remains virtually unchanged from when it was built in the 1920s. Boxes are stacked in echo-filled corridors and the blenders, sorters, rollers, colour graders, labellers, packers and supervisors work in rooms originally designed for sleeping or eating in. Seventy per cent of the workers are women, some with stogies on the go, and the atmosphere is one of toil and gossip. Above all though, El Laguito feels happy.

'That is what they tell me,' says Emilia Tamayo, director of El Laguito since 1994 and the first woman to gain control of a Habanos cigar factory. 'This is a general feeling. All the foreigners who visit us have the same sensation. They talk about the happiness of the people they see here, the look of the workers...

'The factory was created by our Commander In Chief and it was made with the idea of giving jobs to women. I came to work here in 1975. Before then I was a housewife, but I wanted to work, to be useful. The house is the grave of the woman.

'All the rollers used to be women until 1994, when I became director and I started to include men among the rollers. I'm no feminist,' she says, beaming. 'I think that men also have the right to work too...

'We care about our workers. We try to make their lives happy

and help them. Also, there is equal treatment between the directors and the workers. We are different kinds of bosses.'

Perhaps El Laguito has scope for development because it is the jewel in the crown of Habanos cigar factories, and because it is away from the city centre, in a semi-rural setting. Indeed, a new factory is to be built on land adjoining El Laguito and the range of brands and blends is to be extended.

'Very powerful reasons mean we must change and grow,' says Emilia.'It is not a secret that we have legal problems with different brands of cigars. There are companies abroad who want to steal Cuban brands. So we need to bring new brands to the market that are our own and cannot be taken from us.

'I am proud of the Trinidad; nothing is going to take it away from me.'

With the Trinidad and the six sizes of the Linea Classica Cohiba, Emilia Tamayo oversees the production of, arguably, the finest cigars in the world. Yet when the new, slightly milder Cohiba, the Linea 1492 blend, was introduced in 1992 in five sizes to mark the 500th anniversary of Columbus' discovery of tobacco (one for each century), production of this range was allocated to the

Partagas factory in the heart of old Havana. To the serious enthusiast this is hallowed ground; the place of origin of many of the world's best cigars.

Anarchy reigns on the pavement directly outside the Partagas factory, beneath the red neon sign. Workers and friends gather here for a smoke and a chat and cigar-vending hustlers hiss for your attention, pouncing on tourists with offers of discounts on famous brands that would shame a used-car salesman.

Most of the cigars on offer are either fake or stolen and only a fool would be tempted when unlimited stocks of the real McCoy are just a few steps away, on the ground floor of the Partagas cigar store.

Compared to El Laguito, Partagas is a real factory: noise and bustle, rattly service elevators stuffed with people and tobacco, students learning the ropes, heat and sweat, rows of cigar rollers in solitary contemplation of their task, and piles of cigars, all yearning to be smoked. Some shapes, like the vast Partagas Lusitanias double corona, and the pyramid-shaped Montecristo No. 2 (a personal favourite) are familiar, while others like Solomon, an inflated figurado specially commissioned by a German customer, I could only marvel at.

tobacco production

1. The basic hand-rolled Cuban cigar, the benchmark of all cigars, is the sum of three component parts, derived from two varieties of tobacco plants: the *criollo* and *corojo*.

The components are the *tripa* (filler) in the centre; a *capote* (binder) around the *tripa* (both taken from the *criollo* plant); and a *capa* (wrapper) stretched and rolled around the outside (taken from the *corojo*).

Special growing conditions and superlative skills are required to produce the *capa*, the most prized leaf in any cigar.

2. Two varieties of seeds, from the *corojo* and *criollo* plants, are produced at government research stations and, once coated with a protective wax, distributed for planting.

Recently, two new disease-resistant seed strains have been planted: Habana 2000 and Habana 92.

From an October planting, it takes 50 days for plants to reach maturity. Tended daily, the plants' flowering heads and side shoots are removed to stimulate the growth of larger leaves.

3. *Criollo* plants are divided into three sections. The *volada* leaves, the oldest and mildest, nearest the base of the plant; the *seco* medium leaves in the centre; and the most flavoursome, the youngest, *ligero* leaves, at the top.

Corojo plants are grown in fields beneath sheets of muslin, to protect the leaves from direct sunlight and to give them a lustrous, silken appearance, a process called *tapado* (or covering). Eight, sometimes nine pairs of leaves, each with a different name, colour and taste, are picked separately, usually a week apart.

4. All harvested leaves are taken to drying barns, built facing east and west, to shelter their contents from the harmful midday sun. The temperature inside is carefully controlled.

Leaves are sewn into hands of eight and strung on poles (*cujes*) to dry. Air curing takes about 50 days.

The art of the tobacco blender is to combine the *volado*, *seco* and *ligero* leaves with the correct binder and wrapper, to ensure flavour, texture and good burning qualities.

Production of *corojo* is labour intensive and expensive. A good plant will wrap 32 cigars.

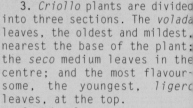

cigar production

1. The leaves are stacked in three feet (1m) high *pilones* and stored at temperatures not exceeding 35°C. Fermentation breaks down resins and creates uniformity of colour.

Leaves are graded for size and colour before a second fermentation. The temperature is checked with sword-like thermometers.

After resting for three weeks, the leaves are packed into bundles called *tercios* and put aside for a few months in the cigar factories for ageing.

2. Prior to rolling, the leaves are gently separated and, in bunches, lightly moistened with high pressure water.

Despalilladoras remove the stems and *rezagadoras* grade the remaining half leaves into size, colour and texture.

The filler comprises three types of leaf (*volado*, *seco* and *ligero*) and throughout the process blenders monitor the progress of each.

Once perfected they are taken to the *liga* (the blending room), where great secrecy surrounds the individual cigar blends.

3. *Torcedores* (rollers) sit at benches, six or more to a row, using a *chaveta* (half moon blade) and a wooden board.

Two to four leaves are combined with the binder and rolled into a bunch, according to the blend.

After pressing in a wooden mould they are wrapped, trimmed and capped using leaf and natural gum.

A good *torcedore* rolls from 120 to 150 cigars a day. These are gathered into bundles of 50 and checked by quality controllers.

4. After rolling, the cigars are placed in conditioning rooms for up to three weeks for the flavours to marry.

Some of the highest paid and respected factory workers are *escogedores* (colour graders). Working at phenomenal speeds they grade the cigars according to colour (65 shades in all) and texture. Others arrange them in boxes from dark to light from left to right.

Cigars are removed from the boxes, for banding, by women *anilladoras*, using a simple measuring rule and gum.

Workers and friends gather here for a smoke and a chat and cigar-vending hustlers hiss for your attention, pouncing on tourists with offers of discounts on famous brands that would shame a used-car salesman.

Located deep in the dark, steaming basement is a tobacco fermentation room; the aroma is stifling. On the first floor I encounter Hilda Chacon, a tobacco grader, who rolls herself a cigar the size of a baseball bat each day when she arrives, wedging the soggy end firmly into her mouth where her front teeth used to be.

If Cuba is to continue to increase its cigar production, new rollers are needed. Ernesto, who is 18, is one of two dozen trainees at Partagas, most still in their teens, who are grappling with the intricacies of rolling. Their target is 150 cigars a day; after seven months, Ernesto is still only on 120. Each trainee is provided with a wooden rolling block and *chaveta*, a half moon blade.

'It is difficult to get on the course. There is a lot of competition and it is hard work,' he says. 'Speed is one thing - it is very important - but the skill lies in combining that with quality, so that each cigar looks and feels and smokes like the last.'

He is learning to roll Partagas corona grandes and laughs out loud at the thought of his first attempt. 'It was a fifth of the quality I can roll now. You could barely smoke it.'

h

he is learning to roll **Partagas corona grandes** and laughs out loud at the thought of his first attempt. 'It was a fifth of the quality I can roll now. You could **barely smoke it**.'

In the top-floor cigar-rolling room of Partagas, a room, like all the others, painted pistachio and brown, I meet Santiago Garcia Perez, a man with a remarkable resemblance to the late Miles Davis. When I offer this observation, he insists he is, in fact, the spitting image of Mahatma Gandhi.

Over the years, the role played at this and other cigar factories by this striking man, now in his seventies, has been crucial. Now retired, Don Perez was a reader whose job, for 50 years, was to read newspaper articles and novels to the workers. It is a service that began in the 1860s and continues to this day. It has even provided the names for top cigar brands: the names Romeo y Julieta and Montecristo are derived directly from two of the most popular stories read in the factories.

'The reader is the one who delivers information and spreads the news,' says Don Perez, relighting his cigar. 'What is read is not a decision of the reader though, it depends on what the rollers and the workers want to hear.'

What is read is not a decision of the reader, it depends on what the rollers and the workers want to hear.

'If they are sad, a reader would read something to make them happy; classical works of world literature. Or for information, they may want to be read to from different news-papers: from France, Spain, Russia, the Czech Republic and England, too. Cubans want to learn it all. The reader is just the bearer of information - the topic is decided by the people - like the director of an orchestra,' he says, through the haze of blue-grey smoke. He contemplates the imagery he has just conjured, and adds: 'Ah, Cuban cigars, such a symphony!'

We had come to Cuba not really knowing what to expect. We had been warned about the bureaucracy by influential men who know Cuba well; the institutionalized slowness of the country and the way nothing ever gets done when, or how, you would like it.

But would I really have wanted it any other way? Whenever our best-laid plans were spoiled, someone would produce a cigar and a light, sometimes a glass of rum too, and then, believe me, Cuba was transformed into the most godly country on earth.

spreading the seed

arturo
fuente
villiger
davidoff
joya de nicaragua
don ramos
royal jamaica
santa clara
santa damiana
macanudo
padron

Many exiled Cuban cigar makers

took their original moulds with them when they left Cuba under Spanish, and later Castro's, rule.

Right: Bunches of filler, rolled and held together with binder leaves, are placed into wooden moulds and mechanically pressed. Once their shape is held, the outer wrapper leaf can be put on.

You are not born with a passion for cigars. Like all the best things in life, they demand patience and determination.

I got my first big chance at an early age... and blew it. My Uncle Ronnie, a Fleet Street journalist, had returned from an assignment in Cuba, then in the first flushes of revolution, and despite my tender adolescence, he stuffed a huge claro claro Havana cigar in my mouth and passed me the matches.

I recall its size vividly, and still half suspect that it was cigars such as this, and not nuclear warheads, that were at the heart of the Cuban missile crisis.

Here was an invitation to an exclusive club called manhood, and all I can remember was turning the same green as the cigar, and throwing up. I didn't care if I never saw another cigar again as long as I lived - until I discovered Eighth Street in Little Havana.

On any afternoon the air here is warm and men in *guayaberas* - short-sleeved cotton shirts worn in the Caribbean -

hang around hole-in-the-wall cafés, sipping syrupy black coffee from tiny plastic cups, and smoking cigars in the casual way GIs chew gum. Noisy old men in Domino Park chomp their stogies into vile, oily stumps and there are so many cigar factories you can smell the sweet odour of tobacco on every corner.

It's the kind of place where anyone is happy to smoke a cigar, freewheeling and easy; where roast-pork smells blend with the sounds of syncopated Latin music.

I push past the brown door of the El Credito cigar factory, and at the small corner counter, in view of the lines of cigar rollers, purchase a pocketful of cigars in all shapes and sizes. Then, I take my place at the counter of the coffee shop on the opposite corner, and slowly and patiently cultivate a new passion in my life: not in the oak-panelled room of a gentle-man's club, nor in the steps of Ernest Hemingway in Old Havana, but right here, on Eighth Street, Miami, Florida, USA.

Cigars have been made and smoked in the USA since the 18th century, possibly earlier. Indeed it was a factory in Conestoga, Pennsylvania, which gave rise to the word 'stogie'.

The cigar makers from Cuba, with their special skills and sacks of prized Cuban seed, arrived later, in two waves: the first during Cuba's struggle for independence from Spain, in the late 18th century. Many leading tobacco growers and cigar makers established themselves in Key West and later, to a greater degree, in Ybor City, near Tampa. By the turn of the century there were 200 factories around Tampa, employing over 5,000 workers, nearly all of them Cuban.

In fact, if you ever find yourself in Whippany, New Jersey (a remote chance perhaps, but you never know) take a peak at J.R. Cigar's high-tech mail order department. Using timbers and fittings from the original Ybor City factories, owner Lew Rothman has constructed a shrine to the founding fathers of the Cuban-American cigar tradition.

That first wave backed the uprising against Spain and in 1895 Cuban hero José Marti (Havana's airport is named in his honour, and his statue stands in front of every Cuban school) led the re-invasion. Details of the attack were delivered to the resistance, rolled inside a cigar, of course.

The second wave arrived, fleeing the Cuban revolution of 1959, and wanting no part either of communism or the Fidel Castro administration.

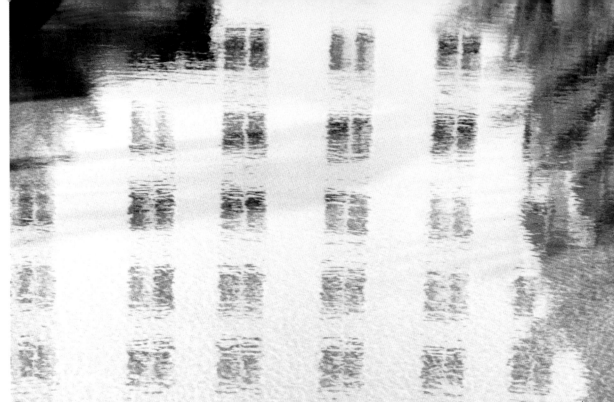

Left: Eric Milon, at The Living Room, believes South Beach is 'like the Côte D'Azur with the American way'.

they may not smoke as many cigars in Miami
as they do in New York, nor have as many uptown settings
to do it in, yet in many ways this tropical city
is much more of a cigar town.

Pages 54-55, 68-71: Cibao Valley — if you want to grow tobacco that
compares favourably with the best from Cuba, this is where to come.
Right: The flowering heads of the ubiquitous Cuban Seed.

The arrival of the second wave of Cuban cigar makers coincided with a decline in cigar consumption in the USA, in preference for cheaper, machine-made cigarettes. Production in Ybor City was scaled down and, looking for work, some cigar blenders and rollers drifted south to Miami, establishing businesses, and a neighbour-hood, in Little Havana.

You will find local cigar stores in every shopping mall, and dozens of divans in and around the heavily gentrified South Beach - the art deco district of Miami Beach - notably on Lincoln Road. Along Ocean Drive, long-legged girls sell cigars from trays while, a couple of blocks away, The Living Room nightclub host, Eric Milon, has installed a cigar vending machine. A world first!

'When the girl comes over, she has four or five cigars,' explains Eric, above the din. 'They can go from $US8 a cigar to $US30, like a wine list. The point is, you may not want to go up to her and ask for a cheap one... because the girl looks pretty and you don't want to look cheap yourself. No problem.

Go to the machine, put the money in and if you want a good cigar we have Cohibas, but if you want a less expensive cigar you can have it, and nobody will know.'

There are more than 20 small, independently-owned cigar factories in Little Havana and that number is growing. They include El Credito, the Caribbean Cigar Company, Caribbean Connection and the inimitable Moore & Bode.

Unusually, Moore & Bode pay their rollers by the day, rather than by the 'stick'; a small label is used on the cap of the cigar instead of a traditional band; and, in place of cedar boxes, cigars are dispatched in bundles, wrapped in kitchen foil and bubble-wrap. They also absolutely refuse to divulge where they buy their tobacco. If they are unable to get the tobacco they require for either of their two blends - Miami and Flamboyan - they simply do not make those cigars. Moore & Bode are purists, and proud.

'We are what could be described as highly eccentric,' says owner Sharon Moore. 'No fake Latin style; very straight-forward, just clean classics.'

hundreds of cigar factories have
closed in the Dominican Republic,
and eventually there will only
be about 30 left,' says Hendrik Kelner
of Davidoff. 'The important thing
for us to maintain the reputation
we have worked hard since the
1970s to establish, and I do not
want to see that eroded.'

i am taken with the small scale of the operation - in a former corner shop - and the diligence and warmth of the rollers, who look more like dinner ladies than the conventional idea of cigar rollers; no exposed thighs here. But what really grabs my attention, and for me what sets Moore & Bode apart, is its top-of-the-range pyramid cigar: full brass. Shaped like an ice-cream cone, it is 7¼in. long with a 64 ring gauge.

'It's a beautiful cigar,' says Sharon. 'A resident of London, well known for his love of cigars, has some shipped to him from Boston every couple of weeks. For him, the full brass is an excellent mid-morning cigar. If this is his mid-morning cigar, where does he go from there?'

In fact, from a purely historical perspective, the full brass is effectively a more refined and better tailored version of the cigar Hilda Chacon rolls herself each morning, before she begins work at the Partagas factory in Havana. And that monster, in turn, is clearly a descendant of the *tabacos* that Christopher Columbus found the indigenous Indians smoking when he landed in Cuba in 1492.

At the time this encounter was chronicled by the monk Bartolome de las Casa:

'All the men carried a torch, breathing in the heady smoke like incense. A few dry herbs were placed on a dry leaf, which was then rolled up into a tube, not unlike a small musket barrel. This was then lit at one end. They inhaled a type of smoke from the other end with each breath, said to soothe the body and have a pleasant, inebriating soporific effect.'

The Spanish role in the subsequent development of tobacco and cigar production cannot be overstated. It began with factories in the Canary Isles and by the 18th century many more had been established throughout mainland Spain.

To this day, Spain remains the single largest importer of Cuban tobacco in the world and is the cheapest country in Europe, by far, in which to buy premium, hand-rolled Cuban brands. For these reasons, plus the fact that smoking is as much a part of the Spanish psyche as Catholicism, Habanos launched Alejandro Robainas'

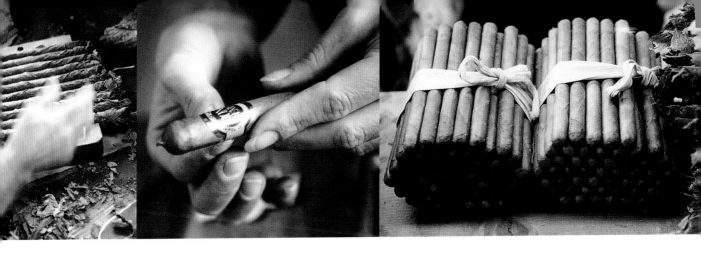

Vegas Robaina range in Madrid in 1997 amid a publicity fanfare befitting royalty.

The Spanish tobacco company, Tabacalera Cigars International, has invested $US367 million in a number of factories and cigar distribution companies in the United States, Honduras and Nicaragua. It now controls 11 per cent of the world market, with a stated ambition to be the biggest and most powerful cigar company in the world.

Tobacco is grown throughout the Caribbean and Central America, and in Florida, Pennsylvania, Minnesota and Wisconsin. Highly-prized wrapper leaf is grown in the humid, foggy valleys of Ecuador, Java and Sumatra (the fog creates a natural canopy), and big investments are being made in the Philippines and Brazil. Cameroon is noted for its dark, sweet wrapper leaf and new land is being made available to growers in India and China. In fact, Alejandro Robaina has been invited to China to advise on planting and production techniques.

It was not the communist revolution in Cuba per se that changed the face of tobacco and cigar production in the Caribbean, although many producers did flee Cuba during that period, taking their skills with them. Rather, it was the subsequent trade embargo - Cubans refer to it still as a 'blockade' - imposed by President John Kennedy in 1962, which changed the industry forever. The big American corporations which had invested there, and many anti-Castro, independent cigar families, found themselves without a natural base to work from.

The effect of the embargo was to deny North Americans the cigars to which they had been accustomed for centuries, and simultaneously to boost investment and production in those neighbouring Caribbean islands and parts of Central America that were already geared up for tobacco.

In many cases they used seed strains taken from Cuba during the post-revolution exodus. Mexico, Honduras, Ecuador, and recently Panama have all been beneficiaries. None, though, has profited from the embargo quite so dramatically as the Dominican Republic, situated just a few miles east of Cuba.

millions of North Americans
have grown accustomed to the milder, smoother smoke from the Dominican Republic.

Right: Tropical flora in the San Juan plantation, Cuba.

Formerly the island of Hispaniola, and now split between the Dominican Republic in the east and Haiti in the west, this verdant, tropical country is the world's biggest producer of premium hand-rolled and machine-made cigars: around 200 million 'sticks', or nearly half the world market. The vast majority of this output is shipped to the USA.

To non-smokers the Dominican Republic represents all that is wrong with cheap package holidays: scruffy, tacky and offering terrible food; entire stretches of the north and south coasts are colonized by anonymous resorts, popular with German and British tourists, where indigenous culture has been reduced to gaily-coloured souvenirs.

The drive south across the Cordillera Mountains, to the city of Santiago de los Caballeros, is a welcome and heavenly contrast: blue-grey mountains as far as the eye can see, and, in the near distance, green, palm-fringed hills. Along the way we pass through villages where old men give toothless grins and children in starched cotton shirts stop to wave and pose for the camera.

No one could describe Santiago as beautiful. The grand Spanish colonial architecture is nearly all to be found further south, in Santo Domingo. Meanwhile, Santiago is anarchic and new, a Third World city full of traffic jams and fumes, dusty streets desperately in need of repair, and noisy bars. Cigar money is pouring in, much of it invested in shopping malls and multi-national burger bars.

The true source of Santiago's wealth lies a short drive to the east, in the Cibao Valley; an idyllic rural backwater, bisected all the way from Santiago to Montecristi in the far north-west, by the Yaqui del Norte River. Hemmed in by mountains on either side, this is the Dominican Republic's version of Cuba's Vuelta Abajo, where, except for the unique orange topsoil, temperature, rainfall and humidity are almost identical.

It could almost be Cuba. Which is why, for decades, growers have been able to duplicate the taste, strength and aroma of Cuban tobacco. Havana devotees, mostly Europeans who have easy access to Cuban cigars, will say they have failed. However, millions of North Americans have grown accustomed to the milder, smoother smoke from the Dominican Republic.

thousands of new acres have been planted in the Cibao Valley and the rarest commodity of all is the cigar roller.

Left: Danny with leaves that will soon be rolled into Arturo Fuente cigars.

The basic process is the same, with subtle differences. Cibao Valley drying barns are lower and wider, some with thatched roofs, some without roofs at all, and some where growers use fires to dry the leaves. And instead of sewing the hands of leaves together, here they are tied into bunches with strips of palm leaf.

Ironically the population here does not have a tradition of cigar smoking; they prefer fags. All production is restricted to tax-free, so-called free zones, from which all cigars are shipped directly to foreign markets. Yet, in the Cibao Valley I came across ragged strands of leaves, strung out along the walls of shanty huts, a sign that things are changing. Perhaps ordinary Dominican Republicans want to discover what all the fuss is about and are having a go themselves.

The unprecedented demand in the USA for Dominican cigars has seen the number of factories rise from a couple of dozen at the start of the boom, in 1992, to around 250 at its height in 1997. Get-rich-quick entrepreneurs arrived in droves, creating blends and making deals with locals who had no experience in producing premium hand-rolled cigars. Before you knew it, the USA was awash with cheap, sub-standard cigars.

Thousands of acres have been newly planted with tobacco in the Cibao Valley and the most-prized commodity of all is the cigar roller. Rolling schools have been established to cater for the demand but factory owners report that their best rollers are frequently head-hunted; others work shifts in two, sometimes three factories.

The largest tax-free zone is a short drive north of downtown Santiago, past the airport and sports stadium, through a shanty town, and on the far side of a set of iron gates where uniformed men search cars and people for contraband. Inside this fence there are over 200 companies employing 40,000 people, producing anything from shoes to cosmetics. There are snack-vending carts on corners and impenetrable iron fences making staff canteens look like prison compounds.

I arrange to visit the American-owned General Cigar factory, where they make the DR Cohiba, Macanudo and Partagas. Nothing remotely romantic here. The factory is run with soulless precision, far removed from anything we saw in Cuba; a large, open-plan workshop, with bales of tobacco entering at one end and boxes of hand-rolled cigars leaving the other.

Just around the corner is
one of the Arturo Fuente
factories, the largest family-
owned operation in the country.
Don Arturo Fuente left Cuba during
the Spanish war, establishing a
cigar factory in Tampa. Since
then his descendants have moved
around the Caribbean - Honduras,
Nicaragua and Puerto Rico -
dodging wars, revolutions and
political upheavals, and settling
in the Dominican Republic in
1980.

From a small workshop with
seven rollers, the Fuentes today
have their own plantations and
employ almost 2,000 rollers.
Their success, primarily in the
USA, is down to a range of superb
cigars standing head and shoulders
above the competition for quality
and flavour. The Fuente Opus X
range is one of only a few
sought-after Dominican Republic
cigars and the family is now
committed to growing all of
its own wrapper leaf, a practice
previously unheard of in
the Dominican Republic, where,
until now, all wrapper leaf has
been imported.

My next appointment is at a
factory partly owned by cigar
legend Hendrik Kelner and the
Swiss-based Davidoff empire,
in another free zone a
few miles away. This factory

replaced an earlier one destroyed by fire in 1996. It is
pristine and white, with the
word 'Davidoff' written in green
scroll along the walls.

Hendrik Kelner has seen
hundreds of get-rich-quick
merchants arrive in the Dominican
Republic, aiming to exploit
the cigar boom in the USA. They
set up hundreds of new factories,
(invariably lacking in the
traditional skills of blending
and production) and employ
untrained rollers. Most ventures
quickly turn sour, and many
of the resultant cigars are
left unsold on the shelves of
American tobacconists. Kelner,
therefore, sees one of his
roles as improving the public
percep-tion of cigars from
his country.

'Hundreds of factories have
closed and soon there will only
be about 30 left,' explains
Kelner. 'The important thing for
us is to maintain a reputation
for quality. Since the 1970s we
have worked hard for it and I do
not want to see that eroded.'

He hopes to achieve this
with an association of Dominican
Republic cigar producers who
have introduced a gold seal of
approval depicting tobacco
leaves, the national flag and
the words *garantia de calididad*

Pages 68-71: Tobacco production in the Cibao Valley: The true source of Santiago's wealth.

- quality guaranteed - to be applied to all leading brands.

'Our other weapon is continually checking and blending,' says Rene Hollenstein, a Davidoff man who has worked closely with Kelner. Davidoff has become a byword for quality control. Their cigars are monitored at eight stages during the production process and Hollenstein smiles when I repeat the rumour that Davidoff rejects more cigars that it sells.

'We continually monitor and check. One way we do this is to smoke cigars made with just one of the three filler tobaccos. This shows us exactly how it would taste if we didn't blend. And believe me, it tastes terrible. The next cigar is made with the second tobacco from the final blend, and the third cigar the last tobacco.

'A fourth cigar contains the entire mixture and then we see exactly what the three components mean in your mouth: one tobacco dries it, the other hurts the tongue - it's too sweet, too salty - and the third is too bitter.

'A good blend will eliminate all the negative parts and only bring in the positive tastes. Like Don Perez, Hendrik calls it a symphony, 'starting with the

violins, then the drums and at the end, the trumpets.'

Until the 1970s the cigar families who departed Cuba and started afresh elsewhere began with totally new brands. It must have seemed to them, since they no longer had access to genuine Cuban tobacco, that they had forfeited the right to use their former brand names. That was until an international court ruled that certain owners retained exclusive rights to their original names, in the USA and elsewhere.

Since then many brands formerly associated only with Cuba have been produced in the Dominican Republic and Honduras. Today there is a dual-nationality Cohiba, El Rey del Mundo, Hoyo de Monterrey, H.Upmann, Montecristo, Partagas, Punch Punch, and Romeo y Julieta The big American tobacco conglomerates are marketing Cuba's cigar mythology, albeit in a different blend and from another country, to a generation of smokers who have not known anything else.

Cuba has responded with new brands of its own: Cuaba, Vegas Robaina and Trinidad, with more certain to follow. Only they have the rights to these brands and, rightly or wrongly, nobody will be able to impersonate them.

b

and on the run: Davidoff spreads the seed.

March 1990. Shock waves reverberate around the international cigar trade. It is the day Davidoff, purveyor of fine Havana cigars for two decades, pulls out of Cuba and shifts its entire operation to the Dominican Republic.

Born in Kiev, and driven out of Russia by the pogroms, Zino Davidoff learnt the tobacco trade in his father's shop in Geneva. He was one of the first aficionados to make a connection between cigars and wine, insisting that both may improve with age. By the end of World War II he had assembled an impressive stock of vintage Cuban cigars. In 1947 he launched his own Chateau collection of cigars, greatly influenced by the Cuban Hoyo de Monterrey brand. In 1969 Cubatabaco invited Zino Davidoff to produce a range of Havanas bearing his name. The following year he went into partnership with Swiss cigar importer Ernst Schneider, and subsequently opened Davidoff stores in a number of major cities around the world. Davidoff's decision to pull out of Cuba, citing poor quality control, and thereby dramatically altering the character and taste of his cigars, upset many customers. But, for all the brouhaha and calls of betrayal, Davidoff remains the biggest independent producer of premium cigars in the world. For sheer rolling perfection, presentation and a balanced, albeit slightly milder flavour, the five Davidoff blends - Aniversario, Number series, Grand Cru, Mille and Special - are hard to beat. Zino Davidoff built a global cigar empire of cigars and designer style, in everything from clothes to cognac. He died, aged 88, in 1994.

If I am completely truthful I have to admit that I went to the Dominican Republic with a feeling, common among European smokers, that no matter how good a cigar may be, whether from here or any other country, if it is not Cuban it can only ever be second best.

A serious and extremely wealthy cigar collector in London once gave me a Fuente Opus X Reserva No. 1, a cigar many in the USA would cut off their right arm for. It was not necessarily intended as a generous gift: rather, it was the act of a man ridding his otherwise perfect Cuban collection of an unwanted growth.

Then I recall the marvellous cigar life in Miami: the mood of the streets, the music, the informal manner in which cigars are enjoyed. And I reach my own conclusion that a cigar's origin is of little significance. It is only the ingredients, the person who made it, and the person who is smoking it that really count. And if by some chance one of the three is Cuban? Well, so much the better, but nothing more.

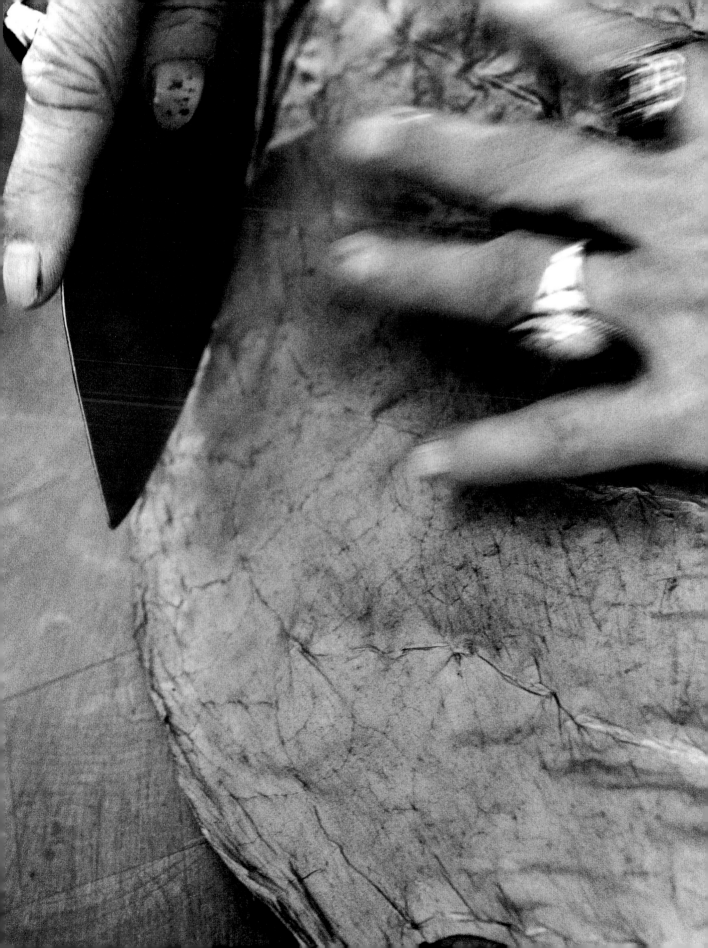

i f I cannot smoke cigars in heaven, I shall not go.

MARK TWAIN

JFK

Nicholson

Clint Eastwood

Orson Welles

Elvis

Arnold Schwarzenegger

Groucho Marx

James Belushi

Che Guevara

John

Alfred Hitchcock

Fidel Castro

Ava Gardner

Huston

Jack

Ernest Hemingway

Humphrey Bogart

power & passion

On stage Orson Welles

would use his cigar almost as others use a cane,
in a repertoire of jousting actions.

In a generation determined to stamp out vice of any kind, cigars are rapidly taking on the symbolism of the Alamo for the resolutely incorrigible. Anti-stogie forces are raging all around and yet, just as all seems doomed for tobacco lovers, another movie icon or supermodel raises a head above the parapet, declaring allegiance to the cigar. Passion or fashion, who can tell?

Nobody was unduly surprised to learn that Hollywood heavy-hitters Arnold Schwarzenegger and Danny DeVito enjoy them. A memorable incident some years ago saw Schwarzenegger being interviewed for *Playboy* magazine. He lit a cigar, then informed the journalist that the interview would terminate when the cigar was finished.

Eyebrows were raised, however, when Demi Moore owned up to a cigar habit. She smokes to unwind and is reported to possess a travel humidor, a gift from fellow cigar travellers Tom Cruise and Nicole Kidman, for the collection of Cohibas she keeps in her trailer when filming. Moore has also been known to dress up in men's clothes and light up, an affectation previously adopted by Marlene Deitrich and the 19th century French female poet George Sand.

Actors Alec Baldwin, Pierce Brosnan, Matt Dillon, Sharon Stone, John Travolta, Isabella Rosselini and Lauren Hutton have all gone public. In the film version of Paul Auster's *Smoke*, Harvey Keitel stars as the owner of a Brooklyn cigar store. The performance was authenticated by a real life passion for cigars which Keitel shares with his friend Robert De Niro.

You only have to read the humidor brass plates in the more renowned cigar clubs to discover who is up in smoke. Those in the Grand Havana Room, Los Angeles, a cigar club for the Hollywood 'cigarati', make for especially interesting reading.

The surest way of establishing your credentials as a romantic, with Latin blood running through your veins, is to smoke a cigar with connotations of Cuba and enjoy long hot humid nights beneath a ceiling of blue haze. That's how Ernest Hemingway played it. He sent Ava Gardner the band from the cigar he was smoking on the night they met.

C
what he was doing Groucho

Challenged by a football referee as to what he was doing with a cigar in his mouth Groucho countered by asking if there was another way to smoke it?

Some enthusiasts have even been prepared to put their money and skills where their cigars are. *Blowing Smoke*, 'a film about guys and cigars,' according to club manager Stan Shuster, was shot in the Grand Havana Room. It's a joint project by several high-rolling members, including director/writers James Orr and Jim Cruickshank and actors Jim Belushi, Stephen Baldwin, Peter Weller, Kevin Pollack, Joe Pantoliano and Joe Mantegna.

Orson Welles rarely went on stage without a cigar, and is even on record as saying that he purposely wrote cigar-smoking characters into his films just so that he could smoke for free. On stage, Welles would use his cigar almost as others use a cane, in a repertoire of jousting actions. On film, as the racketeer Harry Lime in Graham Greene's *The Third Man*, the smoke from his cigar became a sinister and haunting symbol of greed and immorality.

For comedians Groucho Marx and George Burns, puffing on a cigar was a carefully contrived act, allowing their audiences time to get the gags. Burns, who lived to be 100 years old, and who often boasted that he outlived the doctor who told him to quit, has an imprint of his trademark cigar, right next to his hands, in the pavement outside Mann's Chinese Theatre in Hollywood.

If Elvis Presley were alive today, he might have been among the first of the current crop of cigarati to go public. Back in the 1950s and 1960s, the image of the fat-cat cigar smoker was all-pervasive; cigars could not have been less cool. The King understandably maintained his passion for Havanas behind closed doors. He must have taken one look at director Alfred Hitchcock, rarely photographed without a cigar and bowler hat, and decided that that persona was definitely not for him.

The traditional image of the introspective cigar smoker is the epitome of self-containment and contentment, lost in a state of grace, silent in contemplation and enveloped in clouds of aromatic smoke, he inhabits a private place the outside world is unable to penetrate. In such circumstances, momentous projects have been, and continue to be, conceived.

murder, mystery, suspense and a good cigar

- the hallmarks of Alfred Hitchcock.

Meanwhile, the cigar-fuelled contemplations of Ilich Ramirez Sanchez, otherwise known as Carlos the Jackal, have led to the deaths of at least 83 people. Currently serving a 30-year prison sentence, the 48-year-old terrorist, formerly the world's most wanted man, describes himself as a 'professional revolutionary'. He revealed his passion in a letter to French magazine *L'Amateur de Cigare*. As a subscriber he needed to notify them of a change of address - to another high security gaol where he smokes Davidoffs, Cohibas and (well ahead of the rest of the world) Trinidads.

Cigars have oiled the creative cogs of philosophers, artists and composers for centuries. Charles Dickens, Albert Einstein, Sigmund Freud, Ferencz Liszt and Mark Twain were all enthusiastic cigar smokers.

In an odd sort of way, I feel I have trodden in Papa Hemingway's footsteps, visiting his former home on Duval Street, Key West. Later, in Los Angeles, I was presented with an Arturo Fuente Hemingway Short Story, the smallest, noblest and punchiest of a range of premium cigars, produced in the Dominican Republic by an exiled Cuban family. Then, in Paris, I talked cigars with Colin Field, head-barman at the Ritz Hotel's Hemingway Bar. There, between midday and 9.30pm on 25 August, 1944, the author celebrated the Allied liberation of Paris by downing 51 gin martinis. I have also studied his photographs on the walls of El Floridita, another bar in Havana, where they still mix the rum and lime daiquiri that Hemingway drank when his home was in Cuba. At times, it felt as though he had only just left the room and might return at any moment.

For me, the mantle of Mr Cigar goes to British showbiz impresario Lew Grade, now Lord Grade of Elstree. A struggling theatrical agent back in the 1940s, he first invested in a box of cigars to impress his clients, put them in his drawer, and promptly forgot about them.

italian film crews on the classic sixties spaghetti western kept Clint Eastwood's *Man With No Name* supplied with Toscani - the taste of Tuscany. The colour and texture of sun-dried tomatoes, they smoke far better than they look.

I lit up a Havana...and that was the day I was born.

LORD GRADE OF ELSTREE (Right)

One day he lit one up, 'just to see what all the fuss was about,' as he told *Cigar World* magazine. 'And that was the day I was born.' He has smoked seven Montecristo No. 2s every working day since, and proclaims, 'there is still nothing better to put a guest at ease than to offer a Havana cigar'.

Unquestionably the best-known cigar smoker of the 20th century was Sir Winston Churchill. He was voracious, getting through about ten a day. He would smoke in bed until the early hours, with a candle by his side to keep his cigar alight. Friends complained that he left a trail of cigar ash wherever he went.

Churchill favoured a 7in. cigar, with a 47 ring gauge. He would smoke about half its length, the best of it in his opinion, and toss the remainder away. This Havana size is traditionally known in the Cuban factories as a *julieta*. However, in honour of a man who is reckoned to have smoked over 300,000 cigars during his life, many brands have renamed it the Churchill: the benchmark large cigar - the smoke of leadership.

I have always enjoyed the contrast between the image of Churchill - suit and homburg, smoking a cigar, every inch the Western statesman - and those of Cuban revolutionaries Fidel Castro and Che Guevara, in their green military fatigues; men-of-the-people dressed in the colour of the land they fought for.

A lifelong asthma sufferer, Dr Che Guevara nonetheless listed smoking as one of his top priorities. He went so far as to insist that every soldier include a supply of tobacco in his field-pack: 'a companion to a solitary soldier,' he once remarked. I don't know about his powder, but he certainly kept his cigar butts dry so that he could share his smokes with other revolutionaries in the field of war.

Guevara actually started smoking with a pipe, and he only switched to cigars in Cuba (favouring Montecristos, H.Upmanns and Partagas) on learning that Cubans consider pipes to be a gringo pleasure. They called them *cachimba*, as in a Western six-shooter.

I don't drink, I do not smoke, I sleep a great deal. That is why I am in one hundred percent form.

FIELD MARSHAL MONTGOMERY

i drink a great deal, I sleep little and I smoke cigar after cigar. That is why I am in two hundred percent form.

WINSTON CHURCHILL (Left)

This page: Che Guevara
smoked a pjpe in his native
Argentina, switching to the
cigar in Havana when his
revolutionary buddies pointed
out that pipes were for
Yankee gringos.
Left: Fidel Castro smoked
avidly for 44 years, until
his personal physician
insisted he quit.

the power &
the passion of Hollywood.

Cuba's president, Fidel Castro, was an avid smoker for 44 years, until his personal physician insisted that he quit. Castro may have gained some added pleasure from the fact that his former adversary, John F. Kennedy, suffered directly from the USA trade embargo with Cuba he himself instigated.

Shortly after the disastrous American-backed attempt to reinvade Cuba in 1961 (known as The Bay of Pigs) JFK summoned his cigar-smoking press secretary, Pierre Salinger, to the Oval Office. The President told him that he needed a lot of petit H. Upmanns. 'How many', asked Salinger? 'At least 1,000', was the reply, 'and quickly'.

The next day White House officials were instructed to show Salinger directly to the president, the minute he showed up for work. And he had done well. Within 24 hours he had secured for his boss no fewer than 1,100 cigars.

'Good', declared JFK: enough of his favourite cigars to see him through the coming months. Whereupon, he produced a document from a desk drawer and promptly signed it. That was the decree banning the importation of all Cuban products into the USA. The President had taken care of his own needs, then put in place a trade embargo that continues to this day.

It is irrelevant that, for decades, cheap machine-made cigars for the working man and woman have rolled off production lines on both sides of the Atlantic. As far as cartoonists and lampooners are concerned, cigar smokers are overweight and over-paid. Otherwise they are characterized as gangsters - and perhaps with good reason.

Some years ago I worked in a bar on the wrong side of the tracks in south-east London. Each Christmas a crew of north London villains called to pay their respects to a former associate who refused to inform on his accomplices during his years in prison. They were happy occasions, with many Havanas passed around to all and sundry. The only sour note, as I recall, was when one of their younger soldiers produced a Havana nearly twice the size of his boss'. For this insensitivity he was firmly requested to step outside with the offending object.

Gangsters were never so cruel to each other when New York tobacconist Nat Sherman was a boy. In those days, Big Apple gangsters used to call into his father's store in the garment district.

'Bugsy Segal I remember, and some other very famous characters,' says Nat, in the office of his 42nd Street store.

'The thing was, the store was neutral ground. You'd see these limousines pull up and men with bulges under their coats would get out. Guys were out killing each other on the docks, literally, and they'd come in and you'd hear them ask each other what they were smoking. "Let me buy you one," they would say. Cigars are a great leveller.'

unch punch

Right: Big hitter Arnold Schwarzenegger's
preferred cigar is Punch Punch, of course.

Left: Anthony Kiedis of The Red Hot Chilli Peppers, publicly outed for sucking on a stogie on the cover of *Smoke* magazine.

This page: His Latest Flame, the King's secret passion.

the cult of the cigarati is born when Madonna goes public smoking a cigar on US network television.

*Dialogue from an early scene in the Miramax film **Smoke**, written by Paul Auster. Augie (Harvey Keitel) is in his Brooklyn cigar store talking with customers Tommy and Jerry. In walks Paul Benjamin (William Hurt), a local novelist.*

Paul: Two tins of Schimmel-penninck... throw in a lighter while you're at it.

Augie: The boys and me were just having a philosophical discussion about women and cigars.

Paul: Well yeah, I suppose that goes back to Queen Elizabeth.

Augie: The Queen of England?

Paul: Not Elizabeth the Second, Elizabeth the First. D'you ever hear of Sir Walter Raleigh?

Tommy: Yeah sure, that's the guy who threw his cloak down over that puddle.

Jerry: I used to smoke Raleigh cigarettes, they came with a free gift coupon in every pack.

Paul: Well, Raleigh was the person who introduced tobacco into England and since he was a favourite of the queen's, Queen Bessie they used to call her, smoking caught on as a fashion. I'm sure old Bessie must have shared a stogie or two with Sir Walter. Once he made a bet with her that he could measure the weight of smoke.

Voice: You mean weigh smoke?

Paul: Exactly, weigh smoke.

Voice: You can't do that, it's like weighing air.

Paul: I admit it's strange, it's almost like weighing someone's soul. Sir Walter was a clever guy - he took an unsmoked cigar and put it on a balance and weighed it. Then he lit up, smoked the cigar carefully, tapping the ashes into the balance pan. When he was finished he put the butt into the pan along with the ashes and weighed what was there and he subtracted that number from the original weight of the unsmoked cigar. The difference was the weight of the smoke.

t he best way
to break a bad habit
is to replace it with a better one.'

JACK NICHOLSON (Right)

pop stars who have confessed to smoking cigars include Madonna, who appeared on a national American chat show with a cigar on the go; Janet Jackson, who smoked one on stage at an awards ceremony; sometime Spice Girl Geri Halliwell, and U2's Bono. All four members of the the Red Hot Chilli Peppers enjoy a cigar: 'I know it's trendy,' Chad Smith told *Smoke* magazine, 'but I really enjoy them during certain activities - watching the Tyson fight, drinking, gambling.'

Linda Evangelista is said to collect humidors and Eva Herzigova, Kate Moss and Elle MacPherson have all been photographed with cigars. According to a report in *Cigar Aficionado* magazine (August 1997), Claudia Schiffer puffed her way through an assortment of Cohiba robustos and Siglo lVs in addition to two Montecristos (Nos. 1 and 2), during a marathon, five-hour photographic session for a cover article. The supermodel's reward was being voted top cover girl by readers of the magazine.

Cigar Aficionado and *Smoke* magazines have been central to the cigar revival. Both are high circulation, glossy titles, selling hundreds of thousands of copies.

Nothing denotes wealth and status quite so succinctly as a cigar. Aside from an appreciation of the good things in life and the ability to support expensive tastes, the person who wields it also displays a disregard for conventional public opinion and a willingness to take on a modicum of revolutionary chic.

The covers of these magazines (crammed as they are with all the appurtenances of what used to be known as the jet-set lifestyle - fast cars, designer clothes, glamorous accessories) are the perfect place to strike such a posture. And if, in the process, it helps to promote a film, book, record, or career, so much the better.

To paraphrase Jack Nicholson, who got his first taste of the weed whilst filming *The Last Detail* in 1973, the best way to break a bad habit is to replace it with a better one.

Should there ever be an award for the best supporting actor of the 20th century, the cigar will most certainly walk it. Cut... and light.

burning desire

Who are the modern cigar smokers, the new cigarati, the models and musicians, film makers and new-wave bohemians fuelling the cigar boom and filling cigar bars from London to Los Angeles?

My search takes me to London's Notting Hill. On a warm afternoon, two lads in t-shirts and combat fatigues take their pints of bitter and cigars outside a tiny Irish pub to enjoy the sunshine. The pulse of this shabby and chic corner of west London is always a beat or two slower than elsewhere in the capital and the people who live and work here enjoy life at a civilized pace.

Traditionally British pubs are where drinkers smoke cigarettes and fretfully flick ash on the floor. But things are different at Tom Conran's Cow. Behind the bar, a glass case contains hand-rolled Cuban cigars; upstairs, the dining room is the setting for a unique London experience - cigar evenings, hosted by Tom Conran (pictured right).

'A lot of my friends are what I would call part-time cigar smokers,' says Tom, leaning on the bar, 'and the concept of an evening of fine food, wines and good cigars appealed to them. In fact, they didn't need much convincing at all.

These are informal affairs, a far cry from the conventional cigar dinner, with their black ties and pomp. Here men and women, mostly in their 20s and 30s, share a passion for the Holy Smoke. Attending the inaugural dinner was Tom's father, Sir Terence Conran: restaurateur, style guru, publisher, and the man who has done more than most to galvanize new Britain's sense of good taste.

Elsewhere in London, cigar enthusiasts have new places to go - Monty's, The No. 1 Cigar Club, Havana, the cigar bar at Boisdales, and now Che: all of them contemporary settings where smokers can comfortably light up and relax.

Retailers are becoming less po-faced, too. TomTom is a shop and lounge, where people hang out and talk cigars. Owner Tom Assheton came up with the concept whilst soaking in the tub on board his houseboat, moored on the Thames, at Chelsea.

'A lot of people are quitting cigarettes and moving over to cigars,' says Tom, 'and I wanted to offer them somewhere unlike the cigar shops their fathers went to... somewhere less formal, and frankly, funkier. They can have a juice or coffee, play some chess and relax.'

for me, cigars
have changed the nature of
the whole smoking experience.'

BRUCE SMITH, MUSICIAN (This page and left)

24A ▷   **25**   25A ▷   **26**

18A ▷   **19**   19A ▷   **20**

12A ▷   **13**   13A ▷   **14**

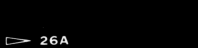 26A 27

 27A 28

 20A 21

 21A 22

 14A 15

15A 16

i think it's the size I love.

JOSEPH ETTEDGUI, right, fashion designer and retailer

Previous page: Twins, Mark and Michael Poish

Since arriving in London's Kensington from his native Morocco in the 1960s, designer and retailer Joseph Ettedgui has had a profound effect on the way fashionable London dresses and eats. He is an advocate of understated good taste, as evidenced by his choice of cigar: the Davidoff Special R, possibly the best looking robusto of them all.

'I think it's the size I love,' he tells me over a cup of coffee in one his restaurants, Joe's Café. 'The Special R is slightly thicker than others. Traditionally when they were thick like that, they would be very long too and that frightens people. A big cigar can be intimidating. Also, I can't have them so long with my height - I'm too short.

'I smoke, on average, at least two or three cigars a day. Always when I am contemplating or when I am quiet at home, watching a video and there is nobody there at all. I always enjoy a cigar more when I am on my own than when I am with a group of people.'

And does he think cigars are sexy? Are they the fashion accessory of the next millennium?

Yes, with reservations: 'Depending on the mood of the photograph. When you think of the cigar you think of the tropics and Cuba and sunshine, and that is complementary. If you wear all white and you have a shoot to do with a straw hat and there is a cigar - it seems very natural. But I don't like it when they use cigars in photographs in magazines just for the sake of it. I think a cigar is something that is quite real and beautiful and not just a prop.'

Right: Australian waitress, Martha Millan, at Cibar, New York.

my search moved on to New York, where Mark Grossich, one of the first aficionados to identify the new smoking trend, established Bars & Books, a dark, mischievously mysterious cigar lounge on Manhattan's upper east side. In his view, sophisticated urbanites in the 1990s have gladly made do with less, only if it happened to be the best.

'They may not be able to buy a Rolls Royce or a bespoke suit, but they can afford to buy a glass of the best single malt scotch and the best cigar, for 20 bucks,' says Mark, whose customers include celebrated cigar smokers Mel Gibson and James Bond actor Pierce Brosnan. 'It gives people pleasure to be able, with not a heck of a lot of money, to feel that they are enjoying something that is truly exceptional.

'People are socializing with style more than ever before. In Britain it's never really gone away, but in America we tend to go from one extreme to the other. One year it's casual, the next year it's formal. But I do think now, that this whole cigar/cocktail lounge thing is here to stay.' The evidence for this is in bars like Cibar, Club Macanudo, The Havana Tea Room, upstairs at Patroon and Pravda.

A ten-dollar cab ride away, drummer Bruce Smith smokes cigars to help him concentrate in the studio. He acquired a taste for Havanas while working in London, initially with former girlfriend Neneh Cherry in Rip, Rig and Panic and later with PiL. He played with the Sade band on their Sweetback project in 1997 and today he lives in East Village, and is in the throes of a Latin fusion project.

We meet, not in one of the many yuppie champagne and cigar bars in and around New York's financial district, but in a place called 7B, on the corner of Avenue B and Seventh Street.

It looks closed from the outside. We are still not convinced it is open as we shuffle through the glass-panelled door into the dark, unlit bar. A man drinks coffee from a white porcelain mug and the humidor, such as it is, comprises a beer glass stuffed with stogies from the Dominican Republic.

'I told you it wasn't chi chi,' says Bruce. 'Nothing fancy. Just a regular local bar for local people.'

Bruce's is a fairly typical story. He likes smoking, but needed to quit cigarettes. 'This guy gave me a cigar and said "try this" and I thought wow, this is a whole other thing. What happened then... for a while, I probably smoked a few too many.

'But soon I found myself smoking less and enjoying it more. Now I go a day or two without smoking and not thinking about it. Instead of it being that kind of neurotic thing - dragging away on the old cigarette - it's an entirely new experience.

'Now, when I'm in the studio, it's something I can take a little time out for - and solve a problem with. It's subtle, and has changed my whole approach to smoking.'

An old friend in Los Angeles e-mailed me about *Twin Falls Idaho*, the first full-length feature film by identical twin brothers Mark and Michael Polish (see pages 120-121). It is the story of Siamese twins, Blake (played by Mark) and Francis (Michael) Falls, and their struggle for acceptance in a hostile world.

On a windswept Santa Monica pier, beneath a fearful sky, Mark, who is 20 minutes older than his brother, explains the crucial scene. It takes place at a Halloween party, where everyone is in disguise and the twins can go undetected, without fear of the ridicule that follows them in public.

'A magician comes up to them and levitates a cigar. He is doing it with his hands and they don't know how. Then the magician lifts the cigar up and places it into one of the twins' mouths. But the twins decide to go one better. 'I inhale and Michael blows out the smoke...

'With Michael and I it is how much we depend on one another for so many things - while at the same time struggling for our own individuality. And yet we are stronger as one because, of course, we were meant to be one - and that is a big theme in the movie.'

By now the word was out that a politically incorrect writer from the UK was in LA, tracking down hip cigar smokers: There was a Colombian sculptor, a transvestite barman, a night-club manager and a plumber! My instincts told me to contact Gabrielle - a 'real rock chick with a passion for stogies', said an informer.

The following day, parked in a side street, in an immaculate 1957 Chevrolet, Gabrielle is somewhat modestly describing herself as a 'sad old Goth' - pale complexion, dark lips, waxy black hair and tattoos. For her, big cigars are the last vice.

'I guess I took 'em up because I wanted to fit in,' she says, fumigating the interior of the Chevy. I want to light up too, but I am afraid that if I do the smoke will be so intense I will lose sight of her. The former presenter of a children's television show, she was fired after an item on body-piercing was deemed unsuitable for infants. Now she manages rock-and-roll bands.

'I don't drink and I don't use drugs,' she confides. 'I cut drinking out years ago - my liver couldn't take it any more - but I wanted to sit at the table and play poker with the boys, and smoke a cigar.

'My friends all think it's disgusting, especially because I only really like big cigars - Churchills, something decent - but it brings me a lot of peace.

'Often people will say to me "What's a little girl like you doing smoking a big cigar?" I hear that all the time when I'm out. But I get the same thing about my tattoos. I'll go into a supermarket in Los Angeles and parents pull their kids close to them.'

late that same evening I am huddled into the open-air smoking terrace of Goldfinger, a nightclub in the centre of Hollywood. It is in the early days of a law forbidding smoking inside any public place - restaurant, bar or club - and being law-abiding citizens, we are dutifully puffing away on a chilly terrace, while all the action is going on inside. The occasion is a birthday party for a girl called Kim, who is wearing a body-hugging, red, sequined dress. Kim runs a baroque-and-roll clothes store on Beverly Boulevard, and appears to be basketballer-tall, in her high heels and hair.

I am here to meet Kristine Lomis. She swapped her cigarettes for cigars, and a small town in New Mexico for the Hollywood music scene.

'To change my life,' she says, 'I had to get out of one-horse towns and dead-end jobs. I dyed my hair, bought a box of cigarrillos and began writing songs. Now, look at me, I'm a Rock Diva.

'Actually, I got the taste for cigars on the Greyhound bus. I was sat at the back with a professor of philosophy. He told me about Cuba and the plantations and how the tobacco leaves are dried and how, when they are ready, they are rolled by hand. He said that such care gives it - the cigar - a spirituality. He called it "chi" and this is what gives us strength. It wasn't the kind of story, or advice, you could ignore.

'People are afraid to smoke here. They even have smoking police - guys who go around clubs to make sure nobody is smoking. You know, I sing with a cigar on stage... not lit, just there, in my hand as a sort of prop, and someone reported that to the manager.

'There is no turning back though, I'm not kicking these, law or no law. This is me, and I like it that way.'

'It's not so rare to see women smoking cigars now,' says dancer Bunty Matthias, 'with Madonna and Sharon Stone making it fashionable. But you still get comments. People seem to thinks it's funny, a woman with a big cigar.'

I confess I raised an eyebrow, too, when I discovered Bunty's fondness for them, solely because Bunty is a ballet dancer. She has her own successful, London-based company, and an energetic lifestyle many

Cigar enthusiasts: Gabrielle page 129,
Bunty Matthias pages 130-131
and Kristine Lomis pages 134-135.

would think incompatible with that of the leisurely cigar enthusiast.

'I like the look of cigars, and the whole production process. I prefer the 4½in., half corona size Romeo y Julietas. Cohibas I find a bit too strong, too heavy.

'For me they are like brandy; I have to be in the mood. I love the 1920s and 1930s and cigars remind me of that period. They seem more elegant than a cigarette. Pulling one out feels novel and glamorous.'

Cigars were never an option for Jake Scott, son of film director Ridley. They are as much a part of his family life as 'camera - action'. I met him in London, in a break from editing his first feature film, *Plunkett & MacClean*.

Jake has a long way to go to rival his uncle Tony Scott, another film director, who has a walk-in humidor in his California home and who gets through up to a dozen cigars a day. But a young man who takes two full humidors with him to the Czech Republic for an 11-week shoot is clearly not some fashion victim jumping on a bandwagon. Jake Scott loves his cigars.

Upstairs at London's Groucho Club, Jake explains: 'My whole childhood has revolved around cigars. For my 16th birthday, one of my presents from my dad was a box of Montecristo No. 4s. My family always encouraged it as an alternative to cigarette smoking, but it can be very expensive.

'It took me a long time to feel comfortable about getting a cigar out in public though, even in somewhere like this. Over the years I have continuously smoked them, but only at home. Now I think it's different because there is such a fashion about them.

'I've searched around and tried different kinds. I like the Hoyo de Monterreys, but these Montecristo No. 2's I still think are the best. The shape is a big part of it... that lovely pyramid shape, tapering at the end.'

And exactly how many did he get through while filming?

'I gave a lot away,' he confesses, with a wry smile. 'It's a good way of getting the crew to like you, and give you that bit extra.

'Whenever we needed another hour of filming after a long day, it would be "Here, have a cigar." It never fails.'

Some people think wearing the right pair of socks can affect the outcome of a game of football. Johnny Vaughan puts his faith in a Punch Punch.

Following page: Eugene Masat from Pravda, New York.

Cigars can even have an effect on the outcome of a football match, or so breakfast television presenter Johnny Vaughan likes to think. Johnny's passions are cowboy films, old Mercedes-Benzes and Punch Punches. These he stores in an 18th century humidor, a present from his girlfriend. To light them he employs another treasured gift - a glass oil lamp.

'It's a kind of cigar light,' says Johnny with typical enthusiasm. 'You get your wick burning nicely. Sometimes I really have had cigars soured by the taste of sulphur on the match, or off a candle or a lighter. But there is something about lighting your cigar with a strip of cedar from the actual cigar box. No aftertaste and you really feel it's the complete Cuban experience.'

His other passion is Chelsea Football Club. Each Saturday he and his friends join forces to smoke their team to victory.

'Three Punch Punches, a couple of H.Upmanns and maybe a Cohiba or two - all belching it out. The stewards really don't like it and we've had a few complaints. I wait until the game is a few minutes in, and I think the team needs a little bit of a lift. The problem is if we've scored a few goals while the cigar has been lit, I have to keep it going.

'You really can delude yourself that your cigar is affecting what is happening on the field of play. Some people think a pair of socks can influence the outcome - for me, it's a cigar.'

Back in Notting Hill, Tom Conran has painstakingly removed the cap of the Montecristo No.2 I have given him.

'Mmm,' he intones, striking a match and savouring the aroma of charred tobacco. 'These Cuban cigars have all been hand-rolled, and you have the sensation that somebody has nurtured the thing... taken time and considerable care.'

He looks up. 'Don't you think they have created a marvel?' Of that, I say, I am quite certain.

a young film director who takes two full humidors with him to the Czech Republic for an 11-week shoot, is clearly not some fashion victim, jumping on a bandwagon. Jake Scott, pictured right, simply loves cigars.

the right stuff

ll a good cigar really needs is a light. There is, nonetheless something compelling about cigar accessories. Crafted with as much care and precision as the smokes themselves, these cherished items - cutters, lighters, cases and humidors - are intimately associated with moments of true pleasure.

Right: Alfred Dunhill solid silver cigar scissors: the surgical way to slice a stogie.

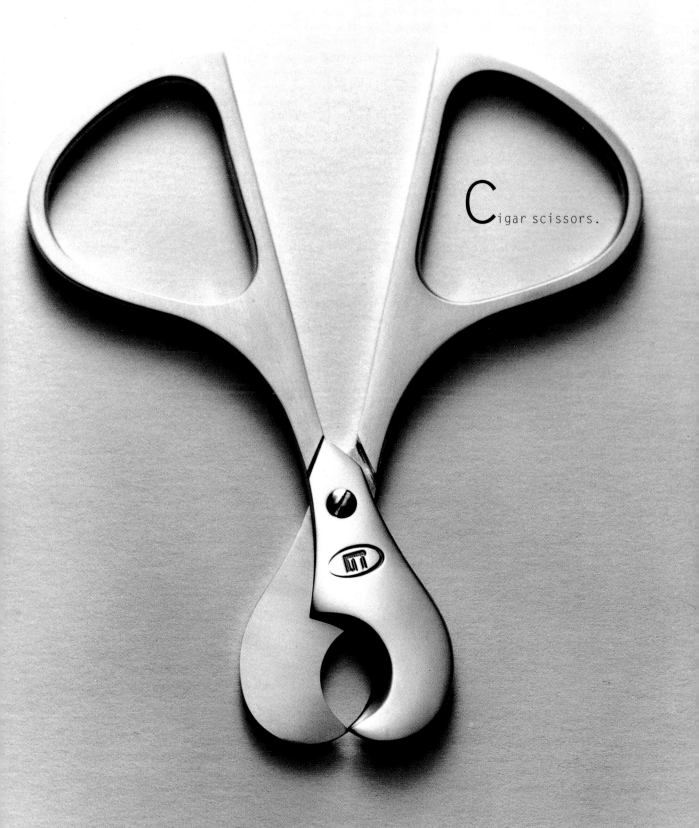

C igar scissors.

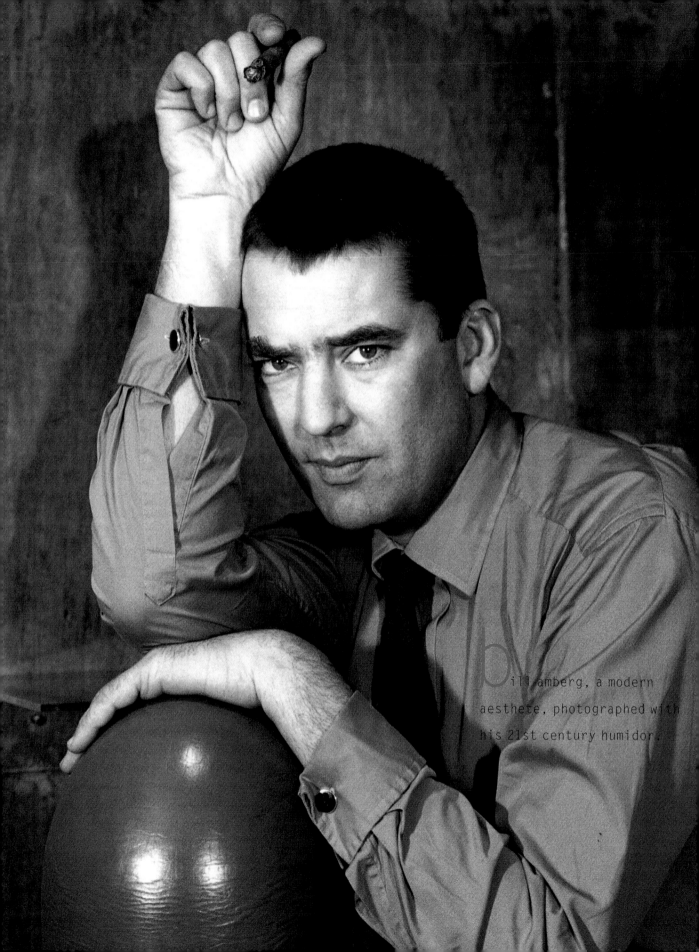

bill amberg, a modern aesthete, photographed with his 21st century humidor.

at rest in a humidor

cigars can be convinced that they remain in the tropics.

To ensure their optimum condition, cigars should be stored at temperatures between 16°C and 21°C, at a relative humidity of 65 to 70 per cent. Even if you are at the North Pole, your cigars will be happier if you can convince them that they, at least, remain in the tropics - Cuba's Pinar del Rio, if at all possible.

Hence the need for a humidor, a solid wooden box, often made of walnut or mahogany, and usually lined with cedar. They are fitted with humidifying units to maintain the correct levels of moisture and temperature inside. These units vary, although a common one, like that in my black, lacquered Davidoff humidor, is an encased carbon 'sponge'. This is clamped to the lid, and topped up with water every few weeks. The lid of a humidor should be heavy and should close firmly, but not too tightly, as a good circulation of air is essential for the cigars to remain 'fresh'.

Cigars can be kept for years like this and the only real danger, then, is 'cigar beetles'. If the cigars become too damp - regulating how much water to use is a matter of trial and error - these tiny pests will bore holes in the contents leaving behind tell-tale traces of dust. If they do strike, don't throw away your entire stock, but try transferring the cigars to a refrigerator for a couple of days. This should kill the beetles. Before you return the cigars to

the humidor wipe down the cedar lining with a clean, damp cloth.

Good humidors are not cheap: £750 to £1000, just for starters. Plexiglass ones are cheaper while really vulgar ones can cost several times that amount. In the long run it pays to have something of quality.

If your habit takes off and you find you do not have enough room for your burgeoning stock, enquire of your cigar merchant about storage facilities. These are also the people to talk to if your cigars have dried out. The patience and skills of a good supplier should be able to breathe new life back into them in time.

Most humidors serve to reinforce the gentleman's club notion of cigars. However, for food entrepreneur Oliver Peyton's latest London restaurant, Mash, designer Bill Amberg threw out all preconceived ideas and devised a humidor fit for the 21st century.

'I designed the humidor with an architect called Andrew Martin, and rather than worry about what people think a humidor should look like, we started from scratch, while keeping the principals of cedar lining and humidification.'

The result is a cylindrical red leather shell which contains a cedar lining and a nickel-plated shelf, for around 100 cigars. Other versions will follow in dark brown crocodile tan, hand-stitched English bridle and Havana leathers.

I once knew a Hungarian poet in Paris who grew the thumbnail of his right hand to around half-an-inch in length and honed the outer edge with a sandpaper file. I remember watching him slip the nail under the cap of his cigar and slowly work it around it, opening the end without loosening the wrapper.

Since then, I have met many people (although without such a precision appendage), designer Joseph Ettedgui among them, who favour this method of opening the capped end of their cigar. Cigars, they say, are natural, organic things, and it is simply too cold-blooded to slice the end off with a steel blade.

Nevertheless, blades remain the single most popular method of 'releasing' a cigar.

The cheapest and most common blade is a simple guillotine in a small plastic holder, which tobacconists usually throw in with a selection of cigars. There are also double-bladed, two-finger cutters; hefty 'V'-shaped cutters designed to remove an eye-shaped wedge; and bullet-cutters employing the same principal as the potato gun, which I had as a boy: a short, sharp-edged tube is bored into the cap, which leaves behind a small cavity when extracted. Knives, table-top guillotines, and special cigar scissors with bevelled edges, are often stored in lids of humidors.

Some of the smartest are circular cutters, designed to be attached to a key-ring or fob-chain. Davidoff, Dupont and Dunhill each make them, at prices from £70.

In the Tabac George V in Paris, I came across a gadget that looked like a miniature corkscrew, designed to be inserted into the shoulder (the closed head or cap) of the cigar several times, according to how much draw is required.

Whichever method you use, it is important to have a steady hand. Cut too far and you risk breaking the fragile connection between cap and binder and the cigar will unravel in your mouth. Too shallow and you may crunch the end together, again restricting the flow of smoke: natural tobacco oils could be funnelled into a small part of the end, which would become sticky and taste bitter.

Cuban tobacco farmers, cowboys and US truckers bite the ends off their cigars. Some people consider this a tad clumsy, not to say risky, particularly when they have paid the equivalent of a decent bottle of Burgundy for a single cigar and would rather smoke it than eat it.

Ultimately, like everything to do with cigars, take care and do it right. After all, have you anything better to do with your time?

For the wrist that speaks for itself:
'Be A Man - Smoke Cigars' cufflinks
from Brooks Brothers, New York.

there are desirable cigar-themed sweat-shirts, ties, umbrellas, barbecue and golf-caddy holders, but *Up In Smoke* would rather invest in a good cigar than any of these. We do, however, make an exception for cigar cuff-links; discretion being the greater part of cigarati style.

When a single cigar can cost as much as a good bottle of wine, it is essential to keep one's stock under lock and key. Customers of Patroon in New York (see Clubbing) are presented with this hefty, bronze padlock to secure their stogies.

tiffany cigar cutters.

Once your cigar is cut, light up. Any match could do the job, but you should be careful to avoid those that are waxed or have a high sulphur content, as these will be detrimental to the taste. Petrol lighters should be avoided for the same reason.

Butane gas lighters are the best. The flame burns evenly and is odourless. Some even have integrated guillotines or cigar punches. Dupont makes a handsome double flame butane lighter in silver or gold, and black lacquer.

The fashion now, particularly among the active set, is for jet lighters: high-tech, high-pressure gas guns with a concentrated blue flame you could weld steel with. Useful, too, should you lose the key to the humidor.

Ashtrays bearing the logos and names of leading cigar brands are very collectable. At the cigar dinner in Havana there was a frantic scrum for the first shipment of large white ashtrays with the name Trinidad.

g ucci ashtray.

how cigars breed new passions

International style guru and restaurateur Sir Terence Conran is a creature of some routine when it comes to smoking cigars.

'I enjoy four a day,' he says, 'and the first is started when I come down to the office in the morning. Someone brings me a cup of excellent coffee, and the first Havana is lit. I love the aroma, the sensation. Smoking is a serious business.

'One of the things I love is the paraphernalia that surrounds cigars. Everything seems very considered and beautifully simple: humidors; big, generous ashtrays; the slivers of cedar that line a good box of Havanas, and which can be used to light your cigar; the yellow ribbon that binds my Hoyo de Monterrey No.2s into a bundle in their box.'

Needing an ashtray befitting his precious Hoyos, Sir Terence turned to Swiss sculptor Christiane Golinelli. She has lived and worked in New York for the past five years and has several of her pieces on display at Quaglinos, one of Sir Terence's London restaurants.

'He wanted something nice to rest a gently smouldering cigar on. He made it sound so poetic,' says Christiane.

'I decided to base it on a shape that I am exploring in all my work - the dome. For me it's an obsessive visual theme, endlessly re-shaped. There is a cradle for the cigar to rest on as it burns and a cup which comes away for the ash.' Both components are fashioned in clay, glazed with terra sigillata, and fired at 1000°C. 'Something to add pleasure to the cigar ceremony,' she says.

A problem shared by all cigar enthusiasts is how physically to transport a small supply of cigars without damaging them. Hefty ones, like Churchills and robustos, may look as tough as old boots, but the truth is they are gentle giants: one false move can unravel months or years of painstaking work.

For most, the solution is an expandable leather case, usually made to hold two, three or four cigars, with a top that slides up and down to accommodate a variety of lengths. The really strong ones have a stainless-steel core.

In the United States a minor industry produces cigar cases for every occasion: for the traveller, with compartments for travel documents and electronic personal organisers; for golfers, that clip on to a caddy and contain golf tees and score sheets in addition to a lighter and cigars. And then there is my favourite, the Nat Sherman Stadium Flask. The ultimate Big Apple accessory: a pewter hip flask and a secret compartment, big enough for a brace of coronas.

However ingenious, they all play havoc with the cut of a jacket.

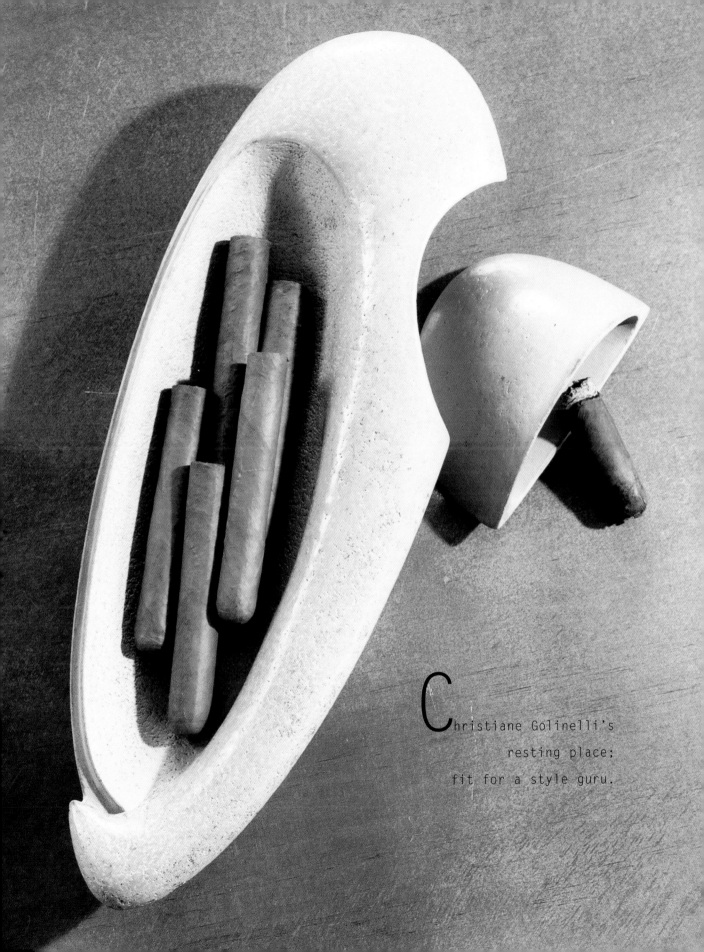

Christiane Golinelli's
resting place:
fit for a style guru.

very cigar smoker should have a couple of tubos cigars like these, with screw-top, aluminium tubes, in their collection,' explains Edward Sahakian of Davidoff, London, picking out a Bolivar No. 1. 'They have a thin cedar lining and when you have smoked the cigar you can always use it again for others. No need for anything fancy.

'However, this is my daytime smoke,' he says with a smile, proffering the small Davidoff Ambassadrice. 'So I had some-thing made that looks almost like a fountain pen that my cigar fits into.' The initials ES are engraved on the side (left).

'Maybe I am smoking and I am called to a plane or I want to go into a shop - I slide my cigar into it and put it into my pocket and it remains there until I have the opportunity to continue smoking. This is my favourite piece of paraphernalia and I always carry it when I travel.'

Fozzie Bear chews on a dog stogie supplied by Celebrity Pets in the USA. Blends include Mutt Donna and Arnold Schnauzernegger. Fozzie Bear, on her home turf in London's Regent's Park, favours the fuller flavour of a Groucho Barks, and, being by nature a rebellious Airedale Terrier, keeps her cigar band on to the last.

bolivar

romeo

el rey del mundo

la gloria cubana

hoyo de monterrey

cohiba

trinidad

vegas robaina

the knowledge

y **julieta**

A little knowledge goes a long way when choosing a cigar. Select the wrong one at the outset and you could end up kicking what ought to be an enjoyable habit, even before it has begun.

Leaving aside, for the moment, characteristics such as flavour and size, cigars are sold in a variety of strengths – from the milder blends, perfect for beginners or as a morning smoke, all the way through to rich, full-flavoured stogies, suitable only for the experienced enthusiast; and even then, only after a rich meal.

This is the era of designer labels and some of the universally known brands are clearly too tempting for the uninitiated. I have met many occasional smokers – birthdays, Christmas and New Year – who light up expensive, full strength Havanas (often large prestige cigars from Bolivar or Cohiba) only to spend the rest of the day staring at the inside of a lavatory pan. Their lesson: that the right cigar in the wrong hands can be a cruel and miserable experience.

O
ften as not

the narrower the ring-gauge

the hotter and spicier

the cigar will burn.

As a basic rule of thumb, hand-rolled Cuban cigars are generally fuller flavoured than those from the Dominican Republic, Honduras, Nicaragua or elsewhere, which tend, for the most part, to be lighter. The traditional Cuban is rich and spicy whereas those from other Caribbean countries, selling in very large numbers to the USA, are far milder.

This is not to say that all Cubans are out of bounds for the novice. H.Upmann and Rafael Gonzalez are classic Cuban brands with extensive ranges any beginner can enjoy, confident that they are smoking something reputable and of real quality.

Edward S. Sahakian, at the Davidoff shop in London's St James's, is frequently asked for advice.

'If you are a beginner and you want to smoke a cigar,' he says surveying the contents of his walk-in humidor. 'I would say try either a mild Dominican cigar, or something mild from the Havana range. I would take you straight to an H. Upmann, or otherwise an El Rey del Mundo. In fact, I have started more people on the H. Upmann Petit than any

other. A small cigar, 4½in. long and quite slim, it will last you at least half an hour. It is mild and a good starting point.

'From there on I would guide a beginner into trying a Montecristo. They are fuller, but fine after a nice meal, with a glass of brandy, or port; or a Romeo y Julieta Exhibition No.3. It's a bit fatter, and 5½in. long, certainly full bodied and full of flavour, but again, not very strong.'

It is worth remembering that all the cigars in a range, produced by the same brand, will have the same flavour, or thereabouts. However, these are all individually hand-rolled cigars, incorporating wholly natural products. Minor variations in the colour and burning qualities are bound to occur. The real differences within a brand, then, are to be found in the length, the girth (called a ring gauge and measured in 64ths on an inch) and the shape. All affect the amount of smoke drawn into the mouth, thereby altering the intensity of what is otherwise a 'brand-constant' flavour.

Note, too, that just because a cigar is long and narrow it is not necessarily any milder, or lighter, than something twice its size. As often as not the narrower the ring gauge the ...

Appearance is very important, and this is an area where many Cuban brands are literally coming unstuck. You may be offered blotchy cigars, some that are split and frayed at the ends, and others where the fine wrapper leaf is coming away. Good retailers are only too aware of quality-control problems and they will usually suggest you sift through a box until you find one you like the look of. In a shop in Havana, I watched a pair of young American aficionados reject a dozen boxes of Punch Punch before they were satisfied.

Do not be too concerned about colour though. The outer wrapper leaf of Cuban cigars provides less than ten per cent of the overall taste and is there for aesthetics and not flavour. It is what is inside and how it is put together that counts.

Search for a cigar with a smooth, even surface, without too many visible veins in the wrapper leaf. It should have a light iridescent patina and pleasant aroma. And finally, if it has been stored correctly, and in the right conditions, it should be ever so slightly soft in the centre. Give it a little squeeze, not too much though. If it is hard, or brittle, it will burn unevenly. And by the way, only a fool puts a cigar to his or her ear and listens to it.

As for size, that's up to you. I personally prefer a big smoke; long panetelas with narrow ring gauges and tubby corona grandes and Churchills. I am what may be described as vertically challenged, and there is a school of thought that says you should only smoke a cigar that reflects your size.

'Absolute rubbish,' says Edward S. Sahakian, defiantly. 'A cigar is there to give you pleasure. You should choose and smoke any one that you like. The only thing you buy in proportion to your size is your suit and shirt.'

The sequence in which you smoke your cigars is important, though. I know a man who starts the day with a 7in. Churchill, smoking ever smaller cigars throughout the day and finishing with a half corona before bed. This is because he wants to be wide awake when he smokes his biggest and best cigars, and he is normally too drunk to care when he turns in.

That is far from normal practice. The received wisdom is to start small and light, and build up in size and strength as you go through the day: logical really. You will not extract much flavour from a Davidoff Ambassadrice if you have just finished a full strength Cohiba Robusto. By the same token you will not derive much pleasure from a meal if you have first neutralized your taste buds with a Bolivar corona gigantes.

The trick is to take your time (I can make a cigar last all night), smoke in stages, and always after a meal, however light. Any cigar on an empty stomach can prove fatal, and the objective, after all, is pleasure, not pain.

50 TOP SMOKES

Not necessarily the greatest cigars in the world, nor the most popular, but the cigars recommended to me during research for Up In Smoke. Cigar reviewers tend to use the culinary metaphors favoured by wine tasters, but after a while, they tend to sound alike. Instead, I have chosen to use the cigar industry's own five-point strength grading scale: light, light to medium, medium, medium to full and full.

QUINTERO
puritos

4 ¼ x 29 Cuba

Behind-the-ear-sized, anytime cigar whose chocolate, bark-like exterior belies a soothing, mellow smoke.

H.UPMANN
petit upmann

4 ½ x 36 Cuba

Creamy and smooth; several retailers recommend this as the perfect beginners' or morning cigar. The politically incorrect even suggest it as 'one for the ladies'.

RAFAEL GONZALEZ
très petit lonsdale

4 ½ x 40 Cuba

I was not prepared for the earthy, almost farmyard flavours of this complex and highly respected cigar, nor for the concentration required to keep it alight.

H.UPMANN
petit corona

5 x 42 Cuba

Light, but with bite. Tightly rolled in an appealing greenish/brown wrapper, with a firm draw, and surprisingly rich for one so mild.

MACANUDO
vintage no.111

5 ⁹/₁₆ x 43 Jamaica

Once a firm favourite in the UK and today the best-selling brand in the USA. A smooth, creamy everyday smoke.

CASA BLANCA
de luxe

6 x 50 Dominican Republic.

A lamb in wolfs' clothing. Not the bruiser the slightly oily Mexican oscuro wrapper suggests. Instead, a sweet daytime smoke with an attractive, brilliant white ash.

NAT SHERMAN
tribeca

6 x 31 Dominican Republic

One of the Manhattan range, dressed in a woody Mexican wrapper, and the ideal alternative to a morning cup of coffee.

ROYAL JAMAICA
corona grande

6 ½ x 42 Jamaica

Traditionally a mild brand. In this 'maduro' size, with a Brazilian wrapper, it has attack and real depth.

DAVIDOFF
3000

7 x 33 Dominican Republic

Exquisitely tailored in claro Connecticut wrapper, and an object lesson in rolling perfection. Cool, almost menthol on the draw, with a light, nutty aftertaste.

SANCHO PANZA
corona gigante

7 x 47 Cuba

Perfect for the beginner looking to impress. Chunky in appearance yet cool, satisfying and undemanding.

MOORE & BODE
no.10

7 ½ x 50 USA

Very impressive, with a mottled claro wrapper, this slightly salty Miami blend, in the double corona size, is subtly satisfying.

EL REY DEL MUNDO
tres petit coronas

4 ½ x 40 Cuba

Wonderfully smooth, instantly appealing, superbly presented. Long live the self-anointed 'king'.

DAVIDOFF
special R

4 ⅞ x 50 Dominican Republic

An iridescent sheen and tasteful white band make this the prettiest of all the robustos. An object lesson in perfection of quality and taste.

EL REY DEL MUNDO
choix supreme

5 x 48 Cuba

Simon Chase, of UK cigar importers Hunters & Frankau, suggested this slightly dry and salty Havana as an ideal pre-dinner, cocktail accompaniment. Right again.

SANTA DAMIANA
seleccion no.500

5 x 50 Dominican Republic

The robusto size of a top-quality range, re-introduced during the mid-90s, with a fuller flavour, and aimed at European smokers with their penchant for spicy Havanas. An unqualified success.

PAUL GARMIRIAN
robusto

5 x 50 Dominican Republic

This feels fabulous; tightly rolled and sturdy. Impeccably cut and an excellent, aromatic daytime smoke that really develops and involves with time.

PAUL GARMIRIAN
belicoso

6 ½ x 52 Dominican Republic

A case of a cigar connoisseur and author putting his own stogies where his mouth is. His achievement? A top quality Dominican that smokes like a Cuban. Very tasty.

ARTURO FUENTE
reserva no.1

6 ⁵/₈ x 44 Dominican Republic

One of the limited edition Opus X range, and rarer than hens' teeth. A complex, engaging smoke with an oily, almost antique wrapper, containing a symphony of sweet spices.

JOYO DE NICARAGUA
no.10

6 ¹/₂ x 43 Nicaragua

Strikingly different and yet extremely enjoyable. A firm, greeny/claro wrapper and a lingering, dry, nutty taste on the palate.

ARTURO FUENTE
londsdale

6 ¹/₂ x 42 Dominican Republic

All Fuentes feel solid, like sticks of wood, with a smart, glossy sheen. Few, however, are as neutral and balanced as this.

MOORE & BODE
full brass

7 ¹/₄ x 64 USA

If you can adjust to having something the size of an Olympic torch in your mouth. This is an incredibly smooth cigar that never fails to raise eyebrows, and cause comment, steadily building as it glows.

COHIBA
siglo 1

4 x 40 Cuba

Small in stature but not in strength. When time is tight, this refined anniversary blend provides a hearty blast of pure Havana.

HOME ROLLED PUROS
panetela

5 x 36 Cuba

There is not an adult Cuban alive who cannot roll a cigar. The quality of farm-rolled cigars varies enormously, but they are always delicious. Ask around.

HOYO DE MONTERREY
epicure no.2

4 ⁷/₈ x 50 Cuba

Topping a Cigar Aficionado blind tasting, with 92 out of a maximum 100 points. What a fabulous cigar, too - richly aromatic, with the undeniable taste of coffee and nutmeg. Everyone's favourite robusto.

ROMEO Y JULIETA
exhibition no.4

5 x 48 Cuba

One to aspire to. A demanding, connoisseur's cigar that should not even be considered until after a hearty meal, and only then when it can be given your undivided attention.

PUNCH
punch punch

5 ⁵/₈ x 46 Cuba

I love this cigar, erratic quality control notwithstanding. A balanced, spicy, robust, value-for-money, compelling smoke for any occasion.

EL REY DEL MUNDO
flor de llaneza

6 ½ x 54 Honduras

Lew Rothman, of the J.R. discount cigar empire , declared this the best in his store. When you consider his Whippany, New Jersey outlet is bigger than most aircraft hangers, that is some claim!

LA GLORIA CUBANA
medaille d'or 4

6 x 32 Cuba

Outwardly a bit patchy, but firmly packed and with an increasingly insistent flavour.

COHIBA
siglo V

6 ⁵⁄₈ x 43 Cuba

Tall, not too dark and very handsome. Mellow and aromatic, medium-flavoured and with a palate-friendly, evanescent sweetness. Very classy.

VEGAS ROBAINA
familiar

6 ⁶⁄₁₆ x 42 Cuba

Bearing the name of Cuba's most celebrated tobacco grower, a class act; a deceptively rustic appearance, bursting with dark chocolate and oozing sophistication.

LA GLORIA CUBANA
tainos

7 x 47 Cuba

A genuine all-rounder. Without the seductive sheen of more prestigious Churchills, it succeeds with that winning combination of medium strength and full flavour.

ROMEO Y JULIETA
churchill

7 x 47 Cuba

Not entirely evocative of the Bulldog Breed, being the light side of medium, but a substantial, stately and consistently cool smoke.

HOYO DE MONTERREY
double corona

7 ⁵⁄₈ x 49 Cuba

Pure refinement and unsurpassed smoking pleasure. Best enjoyed in total isolation, wherein nothing can detract from the soft, mildly-spiced flavours and the lingering, fragrant aftertaste.

CUABA
generosos

5 ¼ x 42 Cuba

The world's first retro cigar, launched in 1996 and intended to appeal to British traditionalists who hanker for something a bit different. Provides a pleasant, aromatic smoke, not unlike a pipe.

COHIBA
robusto

4 ⁷⁄₈ x 50 Cuba

Deserving every bit of praise heaped upon it. A tight, shiny, oily wrapper, an effortless draw and bags of spice. The benchmark medium- to-full robusto.

MONTECRISTO
No.2

6 ⅛ x 52 Cuba

The brand's distinctive spiciness is intensified by the pyramid shape. One of the great cigars, if you can find one that is not falling apart.

HOYO DE MONTERREY
le hoyo des dieux

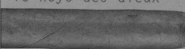

6 x 42 Cuba

The French magazine L'Amateur de Cigare rated this the best of all the Hoyos. Cut to perfection, complex, aromatic - leather and chocolate - and thoroughly absorbing. Heavenly indeed!

NAT SHERMAN
algonquin

6 ¾ x 43 Dominican Republic

A terrific, full-flavoured fruity cigar that continues to develop and satisfy during the 90 minutes or so it is alight.

MONTECRISTO
especial

7 ½ x 38 Cuba

A box of these was my constant companion in Cuba. The shape to supersede the robusto perhaps - the same size as a Cohiba lancero. Perfectly-weighted, with a warm, steady burn.

COHIBA
esplendido

7 x 47 Cuba

Bags of medium-flavour character. As unputdownable as a favourite book. Clear your diary before lighting up and give it the attention it deserves.

DON RAMOS
no.11

6 ¾ x 47 Honduras

Without the soft, aromatic aftertaste of the best Cubans, its greeny/claro wrapper is at variance with the tawny filler. An uncomplicated, pleasant smoke, nonetheless.

MONTECRISTO
'a'

9 ¼ x 47 Cuba

The flagship cigar of Cuba's most popular brand. A spectacular statement of smoking defiance. Tiers of dark, spicy flavours; it takes three hands just to light it and a full evening to enjoy.

PARTAGAS
shorts

4 ⁵⁄₁₆ x 42 Cuba

Break-time-size with a distinctive, deep, full flavour. Try having an unpleasant thought while you're smoking it. It isn't easy. An aide to pleasant contemplation.

BOLIVAR
petit corona

5 x 42 Cuba

With a sleek, iridescent wrapper, this baby Bolivar punches above its weight.

PARTAGAS
no.4

4 ⁷/₈ x 50 Cuba

Powerful, rich, totally absorbing, like stuffing your mouth with Christmas cake and vintage port. Leaves your taste buds reeling for hours.

SAINT LUIS REY
regios

5 x 48 Cuba

Outstanding. An oily, iridescent wrapper, a slow, effortless, even burn, a delicate sweetness on the palate, and, actually, much milder that its reputation leads us to believe.

PARTAGAS
corona

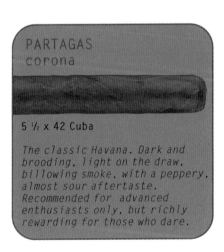

5 ¹/₂ x 42 Cuba

The classic Havana. Dark and brooding, light on the draw, billowing smoke, with a peppery, almost sour aftertaste. Recommended for advanced enthusiasts only, but richly rewarding for those who dare.

MONOPOLI DI STATO
toscani

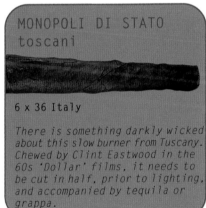

6 x 36 Italy

There is something darkly wicked about this slow burner from Tuscany. Chewed by Clint Eastwood in the 60s 'Dollar' films, it needs to be cut in half, prior to lighting, and accompanied by tequila or grappa.

TRINIDAD
fundador

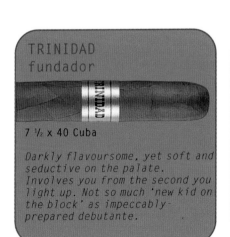

7 ¹/₂ x 40 Cuba

Darkly flavoursome, yet soft and seductive on the palate. Involves you from the second you light up. Not so much 'new kid on the block' as impeccably-prepared debutante.

BOLIVAR
corona gigantes

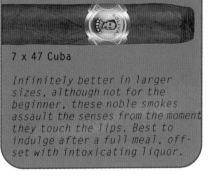

7 x 47 Cuba

Infinitely better in larger sizes, although not for the beginner, these noble smokes assault the senses from the moment they touch the lips. Best to indulge after a full meal, off-set with intoxicating liquor.

How to spot a fake

It's not hard to sucker tourists, particularly in the Caribbean, who may not knowhow to identify a genuine cigar. As the worldwide popularity of premium hand-rolled cigars continues to grow, what used to be a small cottage industry in counterfeits has grown into a major criminal activity.

Fakes are made from unblended, stolen bits of broken leaves. In The Dominican Republic there is not even an attempt to appear genuine. I was offered a box of Cohibas that might have been rolled by a chimpanzee in boxing gloves. The labels and cigars were all different sizes. Slicing the end off one of the contents, whatever they were (not tobacco as we know it), it came apart like a ball of string.

To outwit the counterfeiters and reassure consumers, genuine Cuban cigars carry three hallmarks burnt into the underside of each box. One reads Habano SA, the official Cuban cigar export agency; another 'hecho en Cuba' - made in Cuba - and the third, 'totalmente a mano' - totally by hand. A fourth safeguard is a 4¹/₂in. by 7¹/₂in. green and white government wrap-around seal. Since 1994, boxes also carry a red and yellow Habanos chevron in the top right hand corner.

Sadly, all of these methods are available to counterfeiters who steal them from the factories. This has led some international importers to introduce their own security devices, such as the EMS (English Market Selection) stamp in the UK.

robusto

Holy Smoke. 'The band, though placed around the cigar last,' he writes, 'must always come off first, no matter what bogus connoisseurs might tell you.'

The reasoning is that smoking with the band on is vulgar and horribly *nouveau riche.* By wearing your prestige label you intimidate someone with a cheaper or less prestigious smoke.

To be honest, I prefer to keep the band on because I think it lends character. By the same token I would never attempt to remove the label from a bottle of wine.

If, however, you are a stickler for protocol, do not attempt to tear the band off an unlit cigar, lest you rip the wrapper. Wait until the cigar is lit, and at what the late Zino Davidoff described as its *temperature de croisière* - cruising temperature - and the gum holding the band together has softened.

More controversy surrounds the accumulation of ash, as though the longer the ash the better the smoke. I have seen Wall Street traders holding their stogies aloft, as though breathing through a snorkel, in an attempt to hold on to a tower of ash.

Certainly a firm, even ash, that maintains its shape for an inch or more, is a sign of a well-rolled cigar. Yet there is another argument, that too much ash impedes the flow of air, heats up the cigar, and adversely affects the process of smoking.

Best simply to allow the ash to fall off naturally, in its own good time, and stop worrying about matters of such little consequence.

How to deal with ash

Cigar bands, those intricately embellished paper rings bearing the brand name and logo, were created during the 18th century, initially, so the story goes, for Russian women smokers who did not want to taint their white evening gloves with tobacco stains and smells. But what was a sensible solution 200 years ago is today a matter that openly divides the cigar-smoking community: should the band remain on the cigar during smoking, or should it be removed?

The general consensus comes down heavily in favour of the latter, and is endorsed by author G. Gabrera Infante in his witty and perceptive account of cigars,

Robusto rules! Modern smokers like girth without length. This, some say, is because they don't care for ostentatious cigars; others that they are simply too busy to smoke a corona. Thus, the defining shape of the turn of the century is - the robusto. Traditionally around 5in. long with a 48-50 ring gauge. A pocket-rocket and a sign of the times.

Cape & Volute: a woman's choice

Increasing numbers of female cigarati in Paris are turning to a womens' only club, Cape et Volute. The club meets once a month for a meal and two cigars, and members are drawn from all walks of life, their ages ranging from 30 to 60.

Its president is Valerie Kerever: 'For years I never saw women smoking cigars,' she says, 'and suddenly there are so many; all the French feminist magazines are writing about them.

'Women come to us because we are genuinely interested in cigars, good food and good wine. They take these things very seriously, and are very knowledgeable.'

Seated in Le Fumoir, a popular smoking lounge close to the Louvre in central Paris, Valerie told me about her career in public relations with a champagne and wine company, and how her introduction to cigars was a Punch Punch, given to her by the chef at a promotions dinner.

'Nowadays I like a Sancho Panza Non Plus, essentially a petit corona. It is not too strong, but the perfumes are woody and it burns evenly. The Non Plus is a little, elegant cigar which suits at such times. After an evening meal I treat myself to something more imposing, but still I don't want something too overbearing. The Juan Lopez Seleccion No.1, a corona gorda, is also rather light, but very aromatic. There are subtle flavours on the palate, and an oiliness. I would say that it is a glutton's cigar, or rather, a gourmet's cigar that is big but never over filling...'

(*For details of Cape et Volute and Le Fumoir see Clubbing on page 179.*)

the Ritz, Paris:
top five cigars & cocktails

At the Hemingway Bar at the Ritz Hotel, Paris, head barman Colin Field prides himself on matching the person to the cocktail ('All I need to know is how you feel') and the cocktail to the cigar. These are his top five matches made in heaven.

1. H. Upmann Sir Winston
(also called a Monarcas). Spicy, orange peel, lemon, ginger, coffee and cream, going into pepper and chocolate. With it a Ponsonby - one third cognac, two thirds port over ice. Have it as an aperitif, as an early evening lift. Many less hardened drinkers may prefer it at the end of the evening.

2. Sancho Panza Belicosos
This is a beautiful cigar, with chocolate going into pepper and caramels. Marvellous with a 15-year-old Abelour single malt, with a drop of Grand Marnier. On its own the whisky has a slightly orange smell and if you enhance it with the liqueur you have the classic culinary combination of chocolate and oranges that awakens the palate rather than sends it to sleep.

3. Romeo y Julieta Cazadores,
five to ten years old. A very powerful cigar that begins with pepper, then moves into coffee and something the French describe as 'animal smells', which basically means horse manure. With this the Mk ll Landsburg. Two thirds whisky and one third green Chartreuse and a few drops of fresh ginger steeped in vodka. A powerful end of the evening, a knock-you-for-six cocktail.

4 Partagas Londsdale, Cabinet Selection 50.
An extremely rare cigar. In an old-fashioned glass, pour one tenth Angostura bitters and nine tenths cognac, and lots of ice. This cocktail has the feeling of a Manhattan, but ice gives the cognac a slightly spicy edge which complements the spiciness of the Londsdale superbly.

5 Romeo y Julieta Cedros No. 3.
A cheap cigar, and just the sort to take on country walks, with cedar wood protection so it won't get damaged in your pocket. The finest accompaniment is the dry, smokey, dark Caol Ila whisky. Keep some in a hip flask, and with the Cedros you have the perfect pairing for a brisk winter's walk.

the cigar dinner

To set the mood, a typical evening will begin with aperitif and panetela. Usually there are three featured cigars, the first of these served directly after the main course. It is always the mildest, and smoking is permitted for 10 to 15 minutes, at which time a small savoury dish is served to freshen the mouth and kill the taste of the cigar.

'Doing it this way creates the formality of putting the cigar down and prepares the taste buds for the second,' says Toby Brocklehurst, who holds frequent cigar dinners in addition to arranging cigar tours to Cuba with his company, Special Places. 'You have to do this, otherwise people just keep on smoking and never get to the others.'

The second cigar, often a robusto size and of medium to full strength, is accompanied by cheese and biscuits and coffee. A quarter of an hour is usually long enough for appreciation, whereupon something sweet - a sorbet - is served to freshen the palate once more in preparation for the third and final cigar of the evening - always something a bit special. I attended one of Toby's dinners in Havana where he rounded off the evening with a Sancho Panza Sanchos, a mild, delicious, gentle giant, coming in at a hefty 9¼in. with a 47 ring gauge. It kept me going until the early hours.

'The emphasis is upon tasting,' says Simon Chase, of UK cigar importers Hunters & Frankau. Chase is generally credited with designing the framework for the modern cigar dinners with chef Anton Mossiman.

'At cigar dinners in the USA, as many as six cigars are smoked in a single evening. In the UK we smoke less, and then only after good food and good wine, and, in good company,' he says.

Tom Conran's cigar dinners at The Cow, in London's Notting Hill, attract a fashionable crowd of thirtysomethings (combat fatigues, T-shirts and sneakers, next to designer suits and tousled hair), and his present-ation of the cigars is just as nonconformist. A Hoyo de Monterrey Epicure No. 1 and Cohiba Siglo IV (voted one and five respectively in a *Cigar Aficionado* blind tasting of 94 corona gordas). The third cigar, another Hoyo, the Epicure No. 2, is his father's personal favourite.

'Dig in,' says Tom enthusiastically, breaking with convention and opening all three boxes.

Chef Caroline Perry prepared a hearty feast commencing with terrine of pancetta, foie gras and liver with red onion marmalade. A choice of roast guinea fowl in rosemary salt crust or bouillabaisse with langoustines, crab, mussels and saffron aioli. The meal was rounded off with cheese and apple and celery chutney, followed by tarte tatin.

The wines: a Californian chardonnay, an Australian shiraz and a French white Graves.

Dinner at Tom Conran's The Cow.
Hoyo de Monterrey Epicures Nos. 1 and 2
and a Cohiba Siglo IV: Bon appétit.

Cigar colours

Cigars come in seven very distinctive wrapper leaf shades, from pale green to almost black. Generally, the longer the leaf remains on the plant the darker and sweeter it is, although not necessarily the stronger. Wrapper leaves are grown in Brazil, Cameroon, Cuba, Dominican Republic, Ecuador, Honduras, Nicaragua, Sumatra and the United States. The six basic shades are:

Double Claro: light green to yellow, heated artificially to fix the chlorophyll and increase sugar content.

Claro: blonde, milky brown with minimal flavour.

Colorado Claro: Tawny, mid-brown and aromatic.

Colorado: The classic, grown-in-the-shade, medium brown wrapper with a rich flavour.

Colorado Maduro: A ripe, more intense brown, with a full flavour.

Maduro: Mature, dark, yet often a mild, sweet wrapper with an oily texture.

Oscuro: Dark, almost black as a result of being on the plant the longest.

Cigar shapes & sizes

Unfortunately for the novice there is no easy guide to shapes and sizes. There are over 40 basic Cuban sizes alone and literally hundreds if you include those from other countries.

Cuban sizes range from under 4in. to 9in. in length, with girths or ring gauges - measured in 64ths of an inch - from 26 to 52. However, complicating matters are the manufacturers who use the same names (panetela, corona etc.) but cannot agree on their respective sizes. So, for example, a Romeo y Julieta panetela measures 4⅝in. x 34 and a Cohiba 4½in. x 26.

It is best to use one of the core nine shapes as a starting block. Since they are widely recognized by all manufacturers, any salesperson will know what you are talking about. They are:

petit corona	4in. x 40/42
panatela	5in.-7½in. x 26-38
londsdale	6¾in. x 42/44
corona	5½in. x 42
corona gorda	5⅝in. x 46
double corona	7½in. x 49
robusto	4⅞in x 50
churchill	7in. x 47
figurado	any size

Figurado, tapered at one end, may be called pyramid, belicoso or semi-figurado. The French have their own word, *obus*, meaning canon shell. Those tapered at both ends become figurado or perfecto. However, both are often referred to, rightly or wrongly, as torpedoes. The strangest are *culebra* (pictured left) - three panatelas twisted together and tied with ribbon. Traditionally these were given to cigar rollers in the factories, as a perk. Untied and smoked individually, they did become quite fashionable among avid enthusiasts.

How to smoke a stogie

1. Select a cigar that is slightly springy to the touch, and, unless you want to make a fool of yourself, don't put it to your ear as cigars have nothing to say.
2. Remove the closed/capped end; be careful not to unravel the wrapper leaf. Blacken the other end with a match or gas flame. When it is totally charred, stick the other end in your mouth and light, turning all the time to attain an even glow.
3. Cigars are best enjoyed indoors. Only smoke after a meal, with something to drink, and under no circumstances inhale. Savour the smoke, allowing it to circulate, and take your time: a cigar smoked correctly spends longer away from the mouth than in it.
4. Allow the ash to fall off in its own time and don't panic if it goes out. Simply clean the end with match, and re-light.

clubbing

Davidoff
5 St. James's Street.
tel: 0171 930 3079
fax: 0171 930 5887
A corner store for all cigar smokers' needs, operated with panache by Edward Sahakian.

W.Thurgood
161 Salisbury House.
tel: 0171 628 5437
fax: 0171 930 5887
A firm favourite in the City where high-rollers know how to celebrate; with a Havana from this century-old store, of course.

1

Havana Club
165 Sloane Street.
tel: 0171 245 0890
fax: 0171 245 0895
Smart retail appendage to Monty's - the elegant members club next door.

2

James J. Fox and Robert Lewis
19 St.James's Street
tel: 0171 930 3787
fax: 0171 495 0097
Tom Cruise and Harvey Keitel store their stogies at this 200-year-old tobacconist. The young Winston Churchill opened a cigar account here upon being elected member of parliament in 1900. You can even light up and relax in the great man's favourite leather chair.

Bibendum (2)
Michelin House, 81 Fulham Road.
tel: 0171 581 5817
fax: 0171 823 7925
The flagship restaurant of Sir Terence Conran (1) has the cigar smoking, pneumatic bon viveur, Bibendum, as its symbol and 'Nunc est Bibendum' ('Now is the time to drink') as its motto.

The Leopard Lounge,
The Broadway, 474 Fulham Road.
tel: 0171 385 0834
fax: 0171 385 0862
Glam 70s disco every Thurs, Fri and Sat night, run by cigar smoking twosome Alexis Billson and Howard Spooner (4).

Sautter of Mayfair
106 Mount Street.
tel/fax: 0171 499 4866.
A benchmark retailer located in a fine Victorian gothic terrace in the heart of Mayfair. Good advice and a range of paraphernalia.

Che
23-26 St. James's Street.
tel: 0171 747 9380
Serious aficionados Michael Naylor-Leyland, John Beech and Hani Farsi (3) bring a touch of New York to the West End.

Shervingtons Cigar Merchants
337/338 High Holborn.
tel: 0171 405 2929
Bags of old world character in this mock Tudor store, depicted on the label of Old Holborn tobacco and close to the site of the original factory.

3

4

The Cow
89 Westbourne Park
Road.
tel: 0171 221 5400
fax: 0171 221 7717
Tom Conran (5)
offers oysters and
stout downstairs;
occasional cigar
dinners, for
sophisticated
Notting Hill
bohemians, upstairs.

5

TomTom Cigars
63 Elizabeth
Street.
Tel: 0171 730 1790
fax: 0171 730 1816
www.tomtom.co.uk
Owner Tom Assheton
takes a fresh,
modern, design-led
approach with the
capital's coolest
cigar store. All
the familiar labels
and expertise -
but better dressed.

No. 1 Cigar Club
1 Percy Street.
tel: 0171 636 8141
fax: 0171 636 2826
Opened for just a
year and already
Cigar Aficionado
editor and publisher,
Marvin Shanken, has
a humidor in the
first floor bar.
A sympathetically
renovated town
house with a Cuban
theme, open to non-
members before 11pm.

London

A La Civette
157 Rue Saint-Honoré.
tel: 01 42 96 04 99
fax: 01 42 60 44 78
Recently refurbished, now featuring a walk-in humidor, this Davidoff franchise has been supplying Parisians with Havanas for over 200 years.

La Tabatière
17 Boulevard Montmartre.
tel/fax: 01 42 96 55 94
Informal tobacconist for locals who tend to buy in ones and twos, lunchtimes and after work. An excellent stock of Dominicans for the scooter-riding crowd.

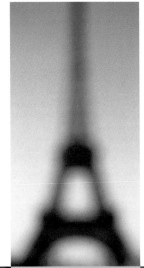

Tabac George V.
22 Avenue George V
tel: 01 47 23 44 75
fax: 01 47 23 84 82
A good selection of pristine Cubans (that's saying something), humidors and the biggest range of cutters I came across on my travels.

Bar Ducasse (1)
59 Avenue Raymond-Poincaré.
tel: 01 47 27 12 27
fax: 01 47 27 31 22
Premier chef Alain Ducasse has added another dimension to his modern interpretation of classic French cuisine, within this exquisite, Art Nouveau townhouse: an English-style cigar lounge. There is a long and tempting selection of vintage cognacs and armagnacs (3) and an imposing pair of glass pyramid humidors, stocked with all the best and biggest Havanas.

Le Fumoir (2&4)
Place du Louvre,
6 Rue de l'Amiral-Coligny.
tel: 01 42 92 00 24
Although I was reprimanded by two non-smokers from the USA, who had not grasped the meaning of *fumoir*, this is a safe haven for cigars. A cool conversational crowd and a library at the back.

paris

Cape et Volutes
3 Cité de Varenne.
tel: 01 45 44 05 89
A women-only cigar
club, run by
president Valerie
Kerever (5), with
frequent and well-
attended dinners.

5

Cubana (7)
47, Rue Vavin.
tel: 01 40 46 80 81
fax: 01 40 46 98 00
Cuban-themed
bar/restaurants are
opening all the
time in Paris. This
excellent one, in
the heart of late-
night Montparnasse,
has the distinction
of serving the best
mojitos (rum and
lemon cocktails)
outside of Havana
and is notable for
its Cuban staff.

8

Hemingway Bar
The Ritz Hotel,
15 Place Vendome.
tel: 01 43 16 30 30
A small, intimate
and surprisingly
local bar, tucked
away at the back
of the hotel. Colin
Field (8), the
English barman,
will design a
cocktail for every
mood and cigar (see
The Knowledge, page
171).

La Casa del Habano
169 Boulevard
Saint-Germain.
tel: 01 45 49 24 30
Jack Nicholson was
paparazzi-snapped,
leaving here with
a handful of Cuban
cigars. I think he
should have lit one
and stuck around and
enjoyed the artistic
ambience of the
downstairs bar and
bistro (6 & 9).

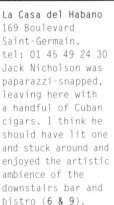

7

9

De La Concha (1)
1390 Avenue of the
Americas,
Manhattan.
tel: 212 757 3167
Lionel Melendi is
Cuban and his
father, who founded
the business, was
a master tobacco
blender. With a
recent doubling of
its retail space,
this hectic, fun,
uptown institution
is 'a zoo' at
weekends, says the
boss.

J.R.Cigars (2&3)
11 East 45th
Street,
Manhattan.
tel: 212 983 4160
Pile 'em high and
sell 'em cheap.
Good value cigars
and paraphernalia
for aficionados,
including owner Lew
Rothman (2), who
can live without
the frills.
Meanwhile, the
Whippany head
office boasts the
largest walk-in
humidor in the world.

Nat Sherman
International
500 Fifth Avenue,
Manhattan.
tel: 212 764 5000
fax: 212 246 8639
Classy smoking
institution,
notable for a range
of cigars named
after Big Apple
icons: City Desk,
Gotham, Manhattan
etc. Light up and
enjoy the piano
lounge upstairs and
Nat's collection of
cigar memorabilia.

2

1

3

Bars & Books (4)
889 First Avenue,
Manhattan.
tel: 212 980 9476
fax: 212 980 9483
007 has lit up in
the cosy back room
and Mel Gibson was
turned away for not
wearing a jacket,
but that's
showbusiness. A
smart, intimate den
of all things nice.
One of the first of
a chain of relaxed,
New York cigar
bars.

4

5

Cibar
56 Irving Place,
Manhattan.
tel: 212 460 5656
fax: 212 460 0011
Beneath the discreet
Inn at Irving Place
Hotel, Cibar is one
of my favourite
places to unwind,
featuring the best
of modern chic,
evoked by waitress
Martha Millan (5),
dynamite vodka
martinis, a terrace,
and well-maintained
humidor. Be warned
though, anything
smaller than a
robusto and you'll
feel underdressed.

Club Macanudo

26 East 63rd Street,
Manhattan.
tel: 212 752 8200
fax: 212 752 7770
Everyone I met said
I had to see this
gentlemanly,
open-to-the-public
'club'. High rollers
and movie stars have
humidors here and
if you wear chinos
and a confident
smile you will not
feel out of place.

Four Seasons Hotel

57 East 57th Street,
Manhattan.
tel: 212 758 5700
fax: 212 758 5711/17
The Fifty-Seven
Fifty-Seven Bar (1),
with a 7 metre
(22ft) high ceiling
and sophisticated
air-extraction
system, is one of
the places for
Friday night
aficionados.

Havana Tea Room Cigar House (2)

265 East 78th
Street,
Manhattan.
tel: 212 327 2012
Eccentric, delight-
ful, theatrical,
Cuban, tranquil,
seductive. Hot tea,
and cigars wrapped
up in satin ribbon
in *fin de siècle*
glass cabinets.
Owner Jeff Tass has
a penchant for black
velvet and enjoys
his cigars with a
minimum of fuss.

Patroon

160 East 46th Street,
Manhattan.
tel: 212 883 7373
fax: 212 883 1118
The glass-panelled
and louvred up-
stairs cigar lounge
is reminiscent of a
1930s ships' cabin
and the brass-
padlocked, wire-
mesh members'
humidors reveal a
collective fondness
for Cuba's
forbidden fruit.
The extensive
Dominican cigar
list includes those
fabulous Moore &
Bode torpedoes from
Miami.

Pravda

281 Lafayette Street,
Manhattan.
tel: 212 226 4696
Seductive, late
night, subterranean
speakeasy, with old
leather furniture
and a feel of old
Russia. Eugene (3)
attends to cigars
(see Burning Desire
p 138) which the
more heretical
customers wash down
with vodka.

new york

Grand Havana House of Cigars
North Canon Drive, Beverly Hills.
tel: 310 385 7700
fax: 310 385 0139
Small yet well-stocked corner shop, directly below the famed club of the same name. Strong links with the Arturo Fuente family, in the Dominican Republic, ensures a steady flow of top-notch cigars.

Kramers
9531 Little Santa Monica,
Beverly Hills.
tel: 310 273 9777
Mrs. Kramer is not impressed by the fashion for cigars (she practically threw me out) and definitely does not enjoy being a tourist attraction. It is worth being barked at, though, for her display of pre-Castro Havanas, the faded press cuttings and other bits of Los Angeles, cigar-related memorabilia.

Beverly Hills Pipe & Tobacco Company
218 North Beverly, Beverly Hills.
tel: 310 276 7358
Quirky and eccentric. There is a range of paraphernalia, old and new, and a small but interesting range of well-priced cigars in the small, walk-in humidor.

Up In Smoke
8278 Santa Monica, Hollywood.
tel: 213 654 8173.
Locals call this a cigar divan, but it is really a shop with a counter to lean on and a scattering of stools. A good place to unwind and investigate top brands from the Dominican Republic (rare Arturo Fuente Hemingway Short Stories) and Honduras. Jeans and trainers and you feel overdressed!

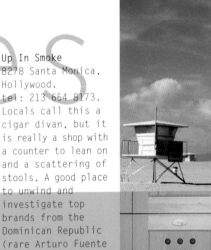

1

Grand Havana Room
310 North Canon Drive, Beverly Hills.
tel: 310 247 2900
fax: 310 474 7475
This big LA pose is rife with stories of Hollywood stars having journalists and film crews tossed out. There is an impressive, curved humidor room (1), behind a wall of glass, although when I called in the waitresses did not appear to know one cigar from another. Related to the original Grand Havana Room in New York (and thus with more showbiz members than a Palm Springs golf tournament), we can expect this benchmark lounge to sire many equally exclusive offspring.

PARKING FOR
BIG EASY
Customers only
IF YOU AIN'T SMOKIN
YOUR CAR WILL BE
TOWED AWAY BY AMATEURS
AND YOU WILL BE PUBLICLY
HUMILIATED
L.A.M.C. 80.71.4

Big Easy - a cigar sanctuary
1922 Westwood Boulevard, Westwood.
tel: 310 234 3279
The neon cousin of the original Big Easy in Studio City; a big, airy, friendly cigar hang out, with leather furniture, books, cold drinks and even a pinball machine. A place for an after-work smoke and read. And how about the large bottle of mouthwash in the rest rooms for customer service?

Wally's Cigar Box
2107 Westwood Boulevard, Westwood.
tel: 310 475 0606
fax: 310 475 1450.
A natural development of the wine merchants next door, Wally's has the distinction of being the only shop, to my knowledge, actually built to look like a cigar box. Among a bewildering array of styles and blends the Rafael (large size only) is their own.

Cigar Connection
534 Lincoln Road,
South Beach.
tel: 305 531 7373
fax: 305 531 0501
It is boom time for
cigars along
pedestrianized
Lincoln Road. Cigar
Connection was one
of the first and is
one of the best,
too. Rosie sits in
the window and
rolls, and inside
there is a wide
selection of their
own Panamanian and
flavoured cigars, for
fashionable South
Beach aesthetes.

**South Beach News &
Tobacco**
710 Washington
Avenue,
South Beach.
tel: 305 673 3002
fax: 305 532 1004
From its beginnings
as a local
tobacconist, this
has developed into
a fully-fledged
cigar divan, with
a branch on Lincoln
Road.

El Credito (4)
1106 South West
Eighth Street.
tel: 305 858 4162
In the heart of
Little Havana, with
the scent of freshly-
roasted coffee on
the breeze, El Credito
is a must. There is
a shop counter
inside the cigar-
rolling *galera*.
Don't expect anyone
to speak English or
to help you choose.
Be decisive and
grab a handful of
excellent Cuban
seed cigars.

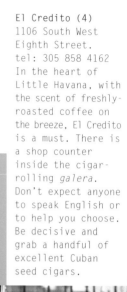

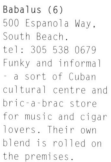

Babalus (6)
500 Espanola Way,
South Beach.
tel: 305 538 0679
Funky and informal
- a sort of Cuban
cultural centre and
bric-a-brac store
for music and cigar
lovers. Their own
blend is rolled on
the premises.

**Cigars Under The
Stars**
Biltmore Hotel,
1200 Anastasia
Avenue,
Coral Gables.
tel: 305 445 1926
fax: 305 913 3159
A Friday night
institution on the
top floor of Miami's
most distinguished
hotel.

Victor's Cafe
2340 South West
32nd Street,
Miami.
tel: 305 445 1313
fax: 305 445 2372
My favourite Cuban
restaurant in Miami
has a cocktail
lounge and cabaret.
Cigars are as *de
rigeur* as
traditional Cuban
guayabera shirts.

5

6

7

9

News Cafe (1)
800 Ocean Drive,
South Beach.
tel: 305 532 4550
Not a cigar club or
divan per se,
nevertheless a
popular place to
sit, smoke and
people-watch.

**The Living Room
at The Strand
(2, 3, 5, 7-9)**
671 Washington
Avenue, South Beach.
tel: 305 532 2340
The hippest place
on South Beach, red
velvet drapes and *fin
de siècle* furniture.
This is a late
night refuge for
beautiful night-owls
and the site of the
world's first
cigar-dispensing
machine.

8

Rehearsals for Club Tropicana in Havana, and the air is heavy with the scent of perspiration and tobacco. Back from their European tour, the 80 or so singers and dancers, in their day-wear, stripped of their sequinned costumes and feather-boa headgear, are working on new routines for what is the world's longest running cabaret. The spicy confection of mulatto beauties and salsa started nearly six decades ago, and the graffiti on the walls of its Bodegita Bar bears witness to those - including Ernest Hemingway, of course - who have succumbed to its exotic, syncopated rhythms. Today they look like regular Cubans, albeit with exceptionally long legs, but tonight - they will shine.

club

tropicana

havana

Casa del Habano (1&2)
Fabrica Partagas, Industria, No 520 Old Havana.
tel: 537 33 80 60
Every aficionado winds up here eventually. There is an impressive selection and an invitation back bar. Look like a high roller, and relax.

Casa del Tabaco Hostel Valencia,
Calle Oficios No53, Old Havana.
tel: 537 62 38 01.
A small, traditional cigar shop, set in the courtyard of a Spanish, colonial-style hostel, shaded by thick, tropical foliage. There is a good selection of cigars on show, but chat with the staff and they may be coaxed into producing the really good stuff.

Casa del Habano
Hemingway Marina, Quinta Playa.
tel: 537 24 11 51 (ext. 2875)
Supplied directly by Habanos, but not as well-known and therefore carrying a much bigger stock and range.

El Floridita 1
Obispo No. 557.
Walk in the footsteps of Ernest Hemingway at Havana's most celebrated bar. Renovated but still packed and a classic place to smoke.

Le Select 2
Club de Cuba, Calle 28, Miramar.
tel: 537 24 10 11
Affiliated to the No. 1 Cigar Club in London. There is a garden, pool, a gym and lunchtime fashion show. Members-only, but invited guests are welcome.

La Veranda (3)
Hotel Nacional de Cuba,
21, Vedado.
tel: 537 33 35 64
fax: 537 33 50 54
Arranged along walls overlooking the ocean, this is simply one of the best bars in the world. There is a cigar shop downstairs and the mojitos are the best.

The Cohiba Cigar Divan

Mandarin Hotel,
Hong Kong.
tel: 852 2522 0111
fax: 852 2520 6528
A Cuban ambience
for this club,
owned by David Tang,
Asia's leading
cigar distributor.

Cheroots Club,(1)

33 Jalan Sri
Hartamas 7,
Sri Hartamas,
50480 Kuala Lumpur,
Malaysia.
tel: 603 653 1633
fax: 603 653 1577
Owner Jeanette Lee
wanted to break
with the conventional
idea of a leather
and wood cigar club
and contacted
London-based
architects GAS-KL

for a solution. A
striking, double-
height glass
construction is the
result, with
humidor and cigar

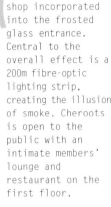

1

shop incorporated
into the frosted
glass entrance.
Central to the
overall effect is a
200m fibre-optic
lighting strip,
creating the illusion
of smoke. Cheroots
is open to the
public with an
intimate members'
lounge and
restaurant on the
first floor.

Gimeno

Ramblas de les
Flors, 100,
Barcelona.
tel: 34 18 49 47
The oldest and best
cigar store in the
city, affiliated to
the city's Epicure
cigar club.
Specializes in
Havanas in addition
to a full range of
Davidoffs.

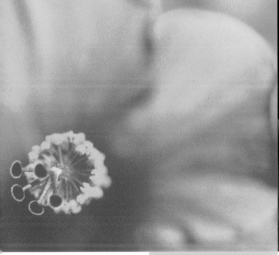

Expenduria de Tabacos

No. 218
Calle Magallanes 16
Madrid.
tel: 34 14 48 33 45
fax: 34 14 46 28 17
The most famous of
Madrid cigar stores
is basically one
large walk-in
humidor; well stocked
with an interesting
and diverse selection
from Cuba and the
Dominican Republic,
plus a full range
of Spanish blends.

Casa Central del Tabaco

Alcala, 44.
Madrid.
tel: 34 15 21 04 20
fax: 34 15 31 05 21
This impressive,
modernist emporium
is the retail wing
of the Spanish
tobacco corporation,
Tabacalera. The
historical links
with Havana mean
there is always an
excellent selection
and expert staff
are on hand to
educate newcomers.

Expenduria No. 74

Barquillo, 22.
Madrid.
tel/fax:
34 15 22 02 22
A traditional store
where the operators,
mother and son,
place the emphasis
on personal service.

'El Club' - de Sigarro Puro Habano,

Calle Serrano, 85.
Madrid.
tel: 34 15 63 76 75
Opened in 1997,
a cigar club with
members' humidors
and a renowned,
traditional Spanish
restaurant.

Club Epicur de Fumadores de Puros,

Balmes 172, 1º 2ª
Barcelona.
tel: 3493 217 30 52
fax: 3493 217 66 84
Frequent cigar
dinners and events
at different
locations and over
500 members at
affiliated clubs
in seven Spanish
cities.

AUTHOR'S ACKNOWLEDGMENTS

People:
Simon Chase, Hunters & Frankau,
London.
Edward Sahakian, Davidoff,
London.
Toby Brocklehurst, Special
Places (Cigar Tours of Cuba),
East Sussex.
Kim Denman at Goddess, Los
Angeles (cover stylist)
Paul Denman, Los Angeles.
Stuart Matthewman, New York.
Versa Manos Publicity, Los Angeles.
Lew Rothman, J.R.Cigars,
Whippany, New Jersey
Fabian 'Fabs' Reyes (our man
in Havana, and team snapper)
Bruno Deffous & Gigi Letts
(our French connections)

Books:
The Cigar Companion, by Anwer
Bati & Simon Chase (Apple).
Le Morane Guide Annuel du Cigare.
The Havana Cigar, by Iain
Crawford (Hunters & Frankau).
*The Connoisseurs' Book of the
Cigar* by Zino Davidoff
(McGraw-Hill).
The Cigar, by Barnaby Conrad
III (Chronicle).
Holy Smoke, by G.Gabrera
Infante (Faber & Faber).

Magazines:
Cigar Aficionado, M.Shanken
Communications Inc., New York.
Smoke, New York, Lockwood
Publications, New York.
Cigar World, London, Hunters
& Frankau, London.
L'Amateur de Cigare, Paris.

Quotations:
Jack Nicholson, from *Cigar
Aficionado* article by Arthur
Marx, Summer 1995. Copyright
© *Cigar Aficionado*. All
rights reserved.
Arnold Schwarzenegger, from *Cigar
Aficionado* article by David Shaw,
Summer 1996. Copyright © *Cigar
Aficionado*. All rights reserved.

Others:
Habanos, Cuba. Virgin Holidays.
American Airlines. National
Hotel, South Beach, Miami.

PHOTOGRAPHER'S
ACKNOWLEDGMENTS

Melvin Cambettie Davies at
Master Mono for his superb
black & white prints and
his insight and guidance over
the years.

The boys at Metro, Clerkenwell
Road - with special thanks
to Brian O'Leary for his
exceptional colour prints.

Sang Choy International,
for their excellent colour
reproduction.

Personal thanks to my
husband, Neil, for all his
support and love. I couldn't
have got through this without
you! And our little boy
Billy, for going without when
the going got tough and for
allowing himself to be bribed
with chocolate cigars.

LB PUBLISHING
ACKNOWLEDGMENTS

There are many people to
thank for helping to get this
project up and running:

- Sir Terence Conran, for
being so encouraging with our
initial synopsis, steering us
in the right direction.
- Everyone at Conran Octopus
Books, especially
Commissioning Editor Denny
Hemming, for breaking away
from the mould and giving us
the chance to produce this
project; Managing Editor
Catriona Woodburn for her
meticulous overseeing and
managing to stay sane; and,
Production Manager Julian
Deeming, a true gentleman,
who saw the proofs through to
a superb standard.
- Jonathan Futrell, for his
original inspiration.
- Lucy Gowans, not only a
design guru but a dear friend
and so inspiring to work with.
- Hilary Burden, for keeping
her steely eye over this
project, & seeing everything
through on an even keel.
- Christina Wilson, our
task master.
- Cheryl Newman, who
assembled an incredible cast
of famous cigar smokers with
such enthusiasm and
dedication.
- Anthony Jayes, for his
wisdom and invaluable advice.
- And, the many people who
have helped and supported all
along the way - thanks guys :
Leslie, Seth , Dixie, Dani,
Daisy, Georgia, Jason, Sean,
Kelledy, Spiney, Ian & Kim.

The Publisher thanks the
following photographers and
organizations for their kind
permission to reproduce the
photographs in this book;
Page 6 Helmut Newton/
Maconochie Photography; **80-81**
Andrew Macpherson/Outline/Katz
Pictures; **83** Nicolas
Tikhomiroff/Magnum; **84** Robert
Capa/Magnum; **87 & 89** Philippe
Halsman/Magnum;
91 PEA/Kobal; **93** Photo
Snowdon/Camera Press;
94 Hans Wild/Life Magazine
(Time Inc/Katz); **96** Elliot
Erwitt/Magnum; **97** Joe
Schersel/Life Magazine (Time
Inc /Katz); **98** Paul
Schutzer/Katz; **100** Burt
Glinn/Magnum; **103** John
Stoddart/Katz; **104** Richard
Faulks/Katz; **105** Michael Ochs
Archives/Redferns; **106** Wayne
Masser/ Visages/Colorific;
108-109 Andre Rau/Sygma;
113 Aquarius Library.

GLOSSARY

cigarillo - small cigar,
traditionally 4⅛in. ring gauge.
claro - medium-brown tobacco.
despalilladoras - leaf strippers.
divan - traditional cigar
lounge.
figurado - bell-shaped cigars,
or tapered at one
or both ends.
humidor - storage case,
commonly of cedar wood,
with relative humidity
interior of 65 to
70 per cent.
maduro - very dark brown
tobacco.
oscuro - black tobacco.
pilones - piles, or stacks,
of tobacco over 1 metre
(3 ft) high.
rezagadores - leaf
sorters/graders.
stogie - generic term
derived from cigars made
in the 19th century in
Conestoga, Pennsylvania.
tabacos - tobacco.
tapado - technique of
growing tobacco beneath
sheets of muslin.
vega - plantation.

WARNING
The Government of the United
Kingdom considers the smoking
of tobacco is and/or can be
harmful to persons smoking
and to third parties. Neither
Conran Octopus Books,
LB Publishing Limited nor
the Author wish to encourage
smoking and do not advocate
or recommend the smoking of
tobacco.

Amberg, Bill, 146, 147
Assheton, Tom, 116, 177
Baldwin, Alec, 82
Belushi, Jim, 86
Blowing Smoke, 86
Bono, 112
Brazil, 63
Brosnan, Pierce, 82,
    126
Burns, George, 86
Cameroon, 63
Caribbean, 63
    Caribbean Cigar
        Company, 58
    Caribbean
        Connection, 58
Carlos the Jackal, 88
Castro, Fidel, 53, 92,
    96, 101
Central America, 63
China, 63
Churchill, 92
Churchill, Sir
Winston, 92, 94-95
Cigar Aficionado
    magazine, 112
cigarati, 82
cigar boom, 8
    choosing, 158-
        169, 170-171
    cutting, 148
    dinners, 116,
        172-173
    humidors, 147
    lighters, 152
    production, 35,
        62, 71
    rolling, 36
Cigar Festival
    Week, 13
Columbus, Christopher,
    62
Conran, Sir Terence,
    116, 154
Conran, Tom, 116, 136
corojo, 34
criollo, 34
Cruise, Tom, 82
Cuaba, 13

Cuba, 10-45
    Pinar del Rio,
        15-18, 23-30
Davidoff, 70, 73
    Zino, 73
    Sahakian, Edward,
        156, 160
De Niro, Robert, 82
De Vito, Danny, 82
Deitrich, Marlene, 82
Dickens, Charles, 88
Dillon, Matt, 13, 82
Dominican Republic,
    46-77
    Arturo Fuente
        factory, 70
    Cibao Valley, 64,
        67,
    General Cigar
        Factory, 67
    Santiago de los
        Caballeros, 64
Eastwood, Clint, 90-91
Ecuador, 63
Einstein, Albert, 88
El Credito, 50, 58
El Laguito, 33
Ettedgui, Joseph, 122-
    123
Evangelista, Linda, 112
Freud, Sigmund, 88
Gabrielle, 127
Gardner, Ava, 85
Gibson, Mel, 126
Grade, Lord, 88, 92-93
Grand Havana Room, 82,
    86
Greene, Graham, 86
Guevara, Che, 92, 97
Habana Libre Hotel,
    13
Habanos, 62
Haiti, 64
Halliwell, Geri, 112
Hemingway, Ernest, 84-
    85, 88
Herzigova, Eva, 112
Hitchcock, Alfred, 86,
    88-89

Hollenstein, Rene, 71
Honduras, 63, 71
Huston, John, 100-101
Hutton, Lauren, 82
India, 63
Jackson, Janet, 112
Java, 63
J.R.Cigars, 53
Keitel, Harvey, 82
Kelner, Hendrik, 70-71
Kennedy, JF, 63, 98-99,
    101
    Bay of Pigs, 101
Key West, 53, 88
Kidman, Nicole, 82
L'Amateur de Cigare, 88
Liszt, Ferencz, 88
Lomis, Kristine, 132,
    134-135
London, 116
    TomTom, 116
    The Cow, 116
MacPherson, Elle, 112
Madonna, 106-107, 112
Madrid, 63
Marx, Groucho, 86, 87
Matthias, Bunty, 130-
    132
Mexico, 63
Miami, 57, 58, 74
    Little Havana,
        50, 58
Milon, Eric, 56, 58
Monroe, Marilyn, 100
Montgomery, General,
    95
Moore & Bode, 58, 62
Moore, Demi, 82
Moss, Kate, 112
Newton, Helmut, 6,7
New York, 126
    Bars & Books, 126
Nicholson, Jack, 112,
    113
Panama, 63
Partagas, 33, 36, 39,
    62
Pennsylvania, 53, 63
Perez, Santiago

Garcia, 39, 44-45
Philippines, 63
Polish, Mark &
    Michael, 120-121,
    127
Presley, Elvis, 86,
    105
Red Hot Chilli Peppers,
    112
Ritz Hotel, Paris,
    88, 171
Robaina, Alejandro,
    14-16, 63
Rossellini, Isabella,
    82, 108-9
Sand, George, 82
Schiffer, Claudia, 112
Schwarzenegger,
    Arnold, 82, 103
Scott, Jake, 133, 140-
    141
Sherman, Nat, 101
Smith, Bruce, 118-119,
    126
Smoke, 82
Smoke magazine, 112
Spain, 53, 62
stogie, 53
Stone, Sharon, 80-81,
    82
Sumatra, 63
Tabacalera Cigars
    International, 63
tobacco cultivation,
    16, 34
    production, 34, 62
Travolta, John, 82
Trinidad Fundador, 13,
    33, 71
Twain, Mark, 76, 88
Vaughan, Johnny, 136-
    137
Vegas Robaina, 13, 62-
    63, 71
Vuelta Abajo, 16
Welles, Orson, 82-83,
    86
Ybor City, Tampa,53,
    58

acknowledgements & index

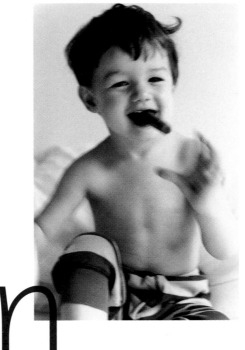

never one for conventions,
Billy Boy chews the end off another Godiva
chocolate cigar - and swallows it.